Praise for Ken Wax

"Ken Wax has a keen teaching ability, and is an inspirational speaker and motivator as well." — *John Dragoon, Novell*

"Ken has deep insight into what it takes to be a successful salesperson in the high tech industry, and is also a phenomenal trainer and mentor. — *Joyce Maroney, Kronos*

"Ken's teachings were instrumental in winning more than 120 new accounts." — *Greg Lazar, ATG*

"I cannot think of anyone who knows more than Ken Wax about working with salespeople – from teaching them basic skills to figuring out ways to overcome the most challenging set of sales obstacles." — *Wendy Stone, IBM*

"Many of our channel partners became millionaires because of Ken Wax." — *Don Bulens, IBM*

"Ken Wax is a salesman's salesman. His expertise and vast experiences in different industries helped my teams exceed our sales targets even during difficult economic times." — *Brian Corey, Monster Worldwide*

"I've hosted over 10 training programs in my career and Ken Wax is the most effective sales trainer I've ever worked with. — *Darren Johnson, Adobe*

The Technology Salesperson's Handbook

114 World Proven Lessons and Tactics

by Ken Wax

The Technology Salesperson's Handbook

114 World Proven Lessons and Tactics

by Ken Wax

Unattributed quotations are by Ken Wax.

www.kenwax.com

First Edition 2011

Printed in the United States of America

The Technology Salesperson's Handbook
114 World Proven Lessons and Tactics

The chapters have been organized in a very specific way.

While you can open to any page and find useful tactics and tools, the chapters are arranged to start with the customer's point of view and how selling has changed, then the best ways and tools for selling to that customer.

Our last chapter is different; it is about personal growth and reaching higher levels.

Chapter 1: **Inside the Mind of the Customer**

Chapter 2: **The New Reality of Selling**

Chapter 3: **It's Called the Sales Process**

Chapter 4: **The Technology Salesperson's Toolkit**

Chapter 5: **Mastering the Meeting**

Chapter 6: **It's All in the Presentation**

Chapter 7: **Advancing to a Higher Version Number**

Contents

Introduction

As of last month, I've led 220 workshops in fourteen countries and consulted with dozens of high technology companies. No two were exactly alike.

My clients include industry giants like IBM, Monster.com, Microsoft, Accenture, and Oracle. Others are much smaller; mid-sized and even startups. Each had the same reason for bringing me in: A key executive knew their team could be winning *more often and faster*.

But that's where the similarity ends.

Some need to outsell larger, well-known competitors. Others *are* those leaders, looking to become more nimble or bring higher performance and consistency across geographies.

Some must get beyond selling to early adopters, others must move up to sell enterprise-wide. You'd be surprised how many need to transform the sales team — their marketplace has become more competitive and now demands new skills.

As I write this, it's impossible to know about you and your specific goals and challenges. That's okay. Whatever they are today, we can both be pretty sure they will be different in six or 18 months. Selling technology is like that.

So in this book I've selected hundreds of specific items from my workshops, magazine articles and keynote speeches. We'll let you choose the ones that are most valuable to you today.

Open this book anywhere to find a chapter that explores some aspect of selling technology solutions. Whether you have hours or just a few minutes, you will find ideas, insights and specific tactics.

- -

Uniquely – and perhaps most importantly – you will also find <u>Words That Work</u>. These are conversations really, ways to put a tactic to work in your interactions with customers. Salespeople around the world have found these remarkably valuable.

In my career I've carried a bag for startups, been a sales manager with a hundred million dollar quota, and held senior executive positions. Open these pages knowing these words, lessons and ideas come from front line, real-world experiences.

If there's one thing I've learned from my work with technology salespeople and executives, it is about leverage. A single change to how one handles a sticky situation can mean the difference between losing or winning a very lucrative sale. Speeding up the sales cycle can literally change a company's future.

It is my hope this book brings you the same sort of impact and results that my direct work has brought my clients.

Ken Wax
Boston, Massachusetts January 2011   www.kenwax.com

How I Got Here

I didn't set out to teach salespeople how to sell technology.
I had no choice.

My technology start was in software sales[*]. I rose into sales management and several of my companies were acquired. When one was bought by Lotus/IBM, I eventually found myself in charge of large sales team responsible for a third of the US with an annual team quota of over $100 million dollars.

My sales team, while a sharp bunch, had limited experience launching and growing into the new markets the company was targeting. That was when I needed to bring in some training. Everything out there, I found, was generic. Every sales training company had models with boxes that prospects were expected to obediently progress through. They offered thick three-ring binders and days full of slide watching.

The closest those generic courses came to addressing my company's goals and challenges was to insert our name in their one-size-fits-all workbooks.

To my amazement, even the group exercises were generic – 'selling' a fictitious product from a non-existent company to an equally non-existent prospect at a fictitious corporation.

For this I was supposed to remove my people from the field for days? Thanks, but no thanks.

---

[*] Before that I was on the other side of the table, as a buyer for Macy's and then in tech distribution with Ingram Micro. I met hundreds of salespeople – and was amazed how little most knew about how buying decisions were made.

So at IBM, I began working directly with my salespeople over lunch and in weekly meetings to discuss our specific situations and to figure out the best approaches for them. It wasn't just talk – we would rehearse real life situations complete with words that would work in those situations (we'll come back to those words in a moment).

This approach led to giving presentations at industry conferences and writing articles about the most effective ways of creating customers. Over the years, as my sales team members moved on and up at new companies, they often invited me in to help advance their teams.

IBM has also brought me back numerous times to train their salespeople and channel partners, give keynotes at their conferences, and to teach executives advanced presentation techniques.[*]

In addition to industry giants, I've also been fortunate to work with many smaller companies. They often have the advantage of being nimble and can seize opportunities quickly; several are used to illustrate lessons in this book.

I ended up teaching thousands of salespeople in seminars, workshops, conferences, web TV and executive meetings in 14 countries on five continents. But as I said at the beginning, it all started because I had no other choice.

It's what I still do today.

[*] Many of which I share in Chapter 6.

How to Use This Book

Notice I didn't say 'read'.

If you enjoy reading, you've picked up the wrong book. Let me recommend John Grisham, Steven King or anything by Malcolm Gladwell.

If you enjoy *selling*, we're both on the same page.

This is the book I wish I had when I was in sales and sales management. It's not a scholarly tome with abstract theories to ponder. Just the opposite – each chapter is filled with real-world approaches that can be used immediately. Each has been field-proven by thousands of technology salespeople at companies of all sizes.

The chapters are short. No lectures, no buzzwords, no modeling what the ideal customer should do. Instead, you'll find page after page of practical ideas and tactics.

Many chapters have Words That Work – examples that you can tailor to your personal style and selling situations. They are clearly labeled.

While most of the topics come from my workshops (a few are from my speeches and magazine articles), there is one thing we do in those workshops that isn't possible in a book: We practice. In no-pressure small groups, each salesperson gets to 'try on' the new approaches and tailor them to his or her own style.

So when you find a topic that is particularly relevant to your next sales call, it's up to you to practice. Bring your own personality to It

----

and envision using that approach with your customers[*]. Then use it and see the impact. Then practice and use another and another and another.

The more techniques you know, the more valuable you become – with more choices for handling whatever selling situations come your way.

[*] Note: You'll find I use the words 'customer' and 'prospect' interchangeably. That's because the line can be fuzzy as prospects become customers, and also because existing customers are the best prospects for future business.

What's the Most Important Thing to Know?

It happens almost every time I fly.

The person next to me asks about my line of work and I tell them I teach technology salespeople new ideas and better ways to create customers for their company.

"Oh, so you know all about technology?" they ask.

My answer usually surprises them. *"No"*, I explain, *"I may know a bit more about technology than most, but what I really know about is how humans in corporations buy – or ignore – technology."*

Selling technology has *never* been about vast technical knowledge. The top sales achievers reached that level by learning more and more about how customers think and what gets them motivated, and also by mastering techniques that create desire and help customers move the purchase along.

The Ugly Truth About Sales Training

Remember the first time you sat through a sales training course?
I do.

The first one was enlightening – a big 3-ring binder and days of slides explaining in great detail a general model of the sales process. There were phrases to repeat and boxes we wanted prospects to step through.

As a beginner I found such structure useful, in the same way a new driver needs to learn how to start a car and pull out into traffic.

Unfortunately, at my next technology company, I had to go through sales training all over again. Another thick binder and long days of almost identical slides and boxes. I learned nothing.

Well, that's not accurate – I did learn not to criticize the training to my boss. After taking us out of the field for days and spending a lot of money, my manager didn't want to hear that it was useless in real-world selling and wouldn't deliver a single change the next day.

I also learned not to ask: *"Hey, aren't our competitors taking the exact same courses?"*

Here's the last thing I learned: Not to ask questions about *our* sale. Politely but firmly, the trainer explained he would be happy to answer any questions we had about *the methodology* – but the course wasn't about our products, our customers or our competitive situations. Learning their model was bigger and more important than that.

I remember telling myself that when I reached sales management positions, I would never take my teams away from selling to turn pages as a 'no questions allowed' reader clicked through generic slides.

When I developed my own sales training courses, I always tailored them to the specific challenges that my client identified. So for Microsoft, I taught their channel partners how to deal with specific current competitive issues and shorten their sales cycle. For Accenture, I taught specific presentation skills. For Monster.com, I created an innovative selling tool and training that enabled their sales force to pinpoint customers' needs and address them.

I would also tailor for the *size* of the technology company. Smaller software or services companies, for example, simply don't have the sort of name recognition that industry giants enjoy. That fact calls for different sales approaches in order to reach the right people and create desire so they'll want to take action.

That's why this book is filled with practical, tactical material.

So while I can't know your company personally from afar, you're likely to find your specific selling challenges addressed as I share with you what has worked for hundreds of organizations.

That's skill training you can put to work for you.

Chapter 1

Inside the Mind of the Customer

Selling technology solutions is the most challenging sales work imaginable. It involves products and services that are complex and often intangible.

It's *always* changing. It's always tempting for customers to wait and do nothing.

But you've done it well enough to be successful. This book is going to build upon all you know.

Let's start by looking 'under the hood' at how things really work in the mind of that customer.

When I teach my workshops, this idea of *'Customer Vision'* is how we start. As thousands of salespeople have discovered, there are unspoken assumptions – about how customers pay attention, learn and come to conclusions – that greatly influence sales success.

What's the View From Across the Table?

If I could grant you one talent in selling – and one only – what would be the most valuable skill you could choose?

Vast industry knowledge? Superhuman technical understanding? Ability to present like a master? No. Plenty of industry experts and techno-wizards are yearning for more customers. As for terrific presenting, that begs the question: What is it that you should say so masterfully?

There is one ability which would be sheer magic. With this skill, and this alone, you could reach new levels of success almost instantly.

I call it *'Customer Vision'*.
If you could somehow peek into the brain of your customer, and check out the view from his or her perspective, your ability to sell would take a quantum leap forward. Because, oh, the things you would know.

You'd know what's important, truly Important to them.
People don't usually tell you this. Sure, they tell you the expected, like, *"We care about price and service and bringing our company a competitive advantage."* Sounds good, sure.

But each of us have goals and desires that never get voiced. It's just not acceptable in business to admit, say, that you desperately want to get that promotion. Or to confess that what is really important to you isn't increasing stockholders' value – it's getting home in time to have dinner with the kids. Our very-human secret priorities drive purchase decisions as much as – and often more than – noble mission statements do. That's a fact of life.

You'd know the best way to proceed.
If you had 'Customer Vision' you'd know precisely who is essential to the decision, and who is mere window-dressing. You'd see potholes to avoid and preconceived notions that need to be addressed. You'd also know when your chances of winning are infinitesimal. So you could cut your losses and move on to better opportunities.

You'd know what you're doing wrong.
In life, we count on feedback to help us improve. In selling, no one tells you if you're botching an opportunity. It's a secret world; no feedback. You learn the outcome, but little else.

Because of this, many salespeople repeat the same mistakes again and again. Too often, people claiming "11 years sales experience", really have only a single year of experience – and have repeated it 10 times.

'Customer Vision' can show you ways to shorten your sales cycle, and how to prevent problems that can undermine your sale.

I hope I've convinced you that 'Customer Vision' can transform your selling abilities. But how do you get it?

Acquiring 'Customer Vision' is not hard, though it does take a bit of courage. You develop it by asking yourself some tough questions throughout the sales process:

- *"How is that customer's perspective on this different from mine?"*

- *"How might they misconstrue or misunderstand this?"*

- *"What matters most to them, regardless of what my company cares about?"*

Then you have to scrutinize your answers to make sure you're not kidding yourself.

It also takes effort. You need to practice the right things. Practice alone doesn't make perfect. Witness the fact that there are many lousy drivers on the road who have decades of experience – as lousy drivers. If you don't somehow bring improvement into the cycle, you end up with well-rehearsed mediocrity.

But it's only hard at the beginning. Once you develop your 'Customer Vision' and begin to use it, you'll find you can now view any emerging customer scenario as those on the other side of the desk see it.

It's a remarkable ability – one that will soon become automatic and almost effortless, and will continually reward you.

The Rational Model and Other Lies

Brainshark seems to be a no-brainer. The company is the market leader in on-demand cloud-based presentation tools for business communications and e-learning.

When their EVP decided that Brainshark should sell enterprise-wide solutions, they needed help learning to sell to higher levels of management.

My two day workshop, similar to one I'd taught for IBM but tailored specifically to their sale, taught them that even top executives won't always make 'rational decisions'.

When we get dressed and go to work, we businesspeople like to believe we act differently from ordinary humans. This is especially true for those involved in choosing technology.

That's why we are all familiar with the 'Rational Model' of decision making. It makes us feel sensible and logical and goes something like this:

> When we have a problem, we begin by investigating all the appropriate possible choices. We carefully analyze each one of them, and map it to our specific, well thought-out needs. Then we're set to weigh our choices, which we do sensibly and objectively. Tah-dah, we arrive at our decision!

What's not to like? Who doesn't want to believe that they and their organization act clearly, carefully, logically, intelligently, and decisively?

This Rational Model is so alluring that many technology companies — filled with very logical and rational folks — have built their sales and marketing approach based upon it. Most classic sales training courses depend on customers behaving this way.

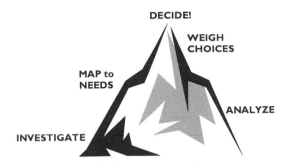

This is the best way to make consistently good decisions. Too bad no one really does it.

The problem with the 'Rational Model' is that it is only a part of the big picture. It may get all the attention, but it's just the tip of the iceberg.

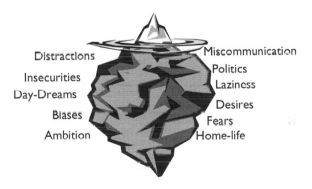

That tiny tip is all they'll talk about, but the driving forces that determine your sale are hidden below.

What Are They Hiding?

The many other factors hidden below the waterline play a big role in decisions – but don't expect them to be discussed very much, especially with salespeople.

For example, who will confess they couldn't focus on your presentation because they've got problems at home or a sore back? Ever heard a contact say that they're planning on leaving the company in two months? Nevertheless, hundreds of thousands of people are in that stage right now. They're just not talking about it.

Somewhere below the waterline, your sale is being influenced. If you're selling to humans, there's no getting around it. Whether your contact is ambitious or cautious is going to impact your sale one way or another. Even clairvoyance enters the picture – how many sales are not going to happen this quarter because a contact has psychically decided their boss doesn't want to hear about such things right now?

There's nothing wrong with believing in the 'Rational Model' – as long as you don't only believe in it. Human nature doesn't vanish when we arrive at the office. It doesn't cease to be a factor just because we don't talk about it during work hours.

If the way you and your company sell ignores these quiet factors, you're going to get surprised as human nature expresses itself. Don't count on them being good surprises.

But if you build for how people truly make complex buying decisions, you won't get surprised nearly as often.

How do you see below the tip? 'Customer Vision' is the answer – seeing the whole person and challenge. Those insights will show you what they really need to grasp and appreciate for your sale to become a priority.

That raises another question: How exactly do customers grasp new things?

How Do People Absorb – or Not?

We tend to take certain things for granted. For example, when we carefully and professionally explain our remarkable solution to others, we expect they will take it all in.

Everything really hinges on whether or not that prospect 'gets it'. If they do, the sale may advance. But if they fail to absorb what is being explained, there's no chance. So let's take a moment to think about this crucial phase in selling.

- *How do people absorb as you talk?*

- *How do they make sense of the many things you talk about?*

- *Where does confusion or boredom come from?*

Your customers have a system. It's pretty much the same one you use countless times every day without even thinking about it.

I call it the 'Listen-Grasp Model' and here's how it works:

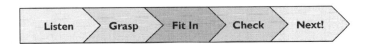

This is the model I teach in my seminars. Try to skip a step and you've got a confused customer and a lost sale.

Let's start with a simple phrase, then we'll spot where problems can enter the picture. Suppose I say to you:

"It's sunny out and the sky is blue."

As I say that, what happens in your mind?

----

1) You <u>Listen</u> and Hear Words

Sound waves come across from me to you. Because you understand this language, you easily turn these sounds into words with meaning to you.

2) You <u>Grasp</u> Them

Now you interpret the context and meaning of my words, making sense of them. Ah, he's talking about the weather, evidently on a clear day.

3) You <u>Fit It In</u> With All You Know

Not a trivial task, but you do it effortlessly. You decide that the most likely reason is that I'm making small talk, or possibly pointing out that the forecast was wrong.

4) You Then Do a Consistency <u>Check</u>

Crucial phase: Does this all now make sense?

For example, if you knew it was pouring outside just a moment ago, you'd need to figure out the disconnect before moving on. This 'Check' stage is a very important one[*].

5) <u>Next</u> You Return to 'Listen' Mode

Your brain is now poised to listen to my next utterance. And the whole cycle begins again.

We're all doing this complex process all the time, for every bit of information that comes our way. Each of us may do it at different speeds, but it's the only way to absorb.

It's easy and quick to do this when the topic is familiar, but complications arise when new ideas or complex topics are being served up.

---

[*] It's also known as a B.S. filter.

Let's look at where trouble can develop. What if, instead, you heard me say,

"It's sunny out and the sky is plaid."?

Whoa. Something is wrong. Either during Step 3 or 4, your lightning fast processing would slow down or even come to a halt. You'd have no choice but to stop and figure it out: Did you hear me correctly? Was I trying to be funny?

So much for the weather. What happens on a sales call if I, a prospect, hear an acronym that I don't instantly grasp?

It's not the end of the world, of course. My mind simply stops the process, at least briefly, so I can figure out what it means. That may only take a second or two. Things get worse, however, if the salesperson continues on full steam while I'm disengaged. It's then hard to catch up. Confusion comes next.

How about if I hear a claim that doesn't pass my Step 4 testing? I may conclude this person is not worth my time and effort. I'll simply stop paying attention.

Now it's time to consider how quickly that prospect can make sense of the information you are bringing him or her.

A Monster Idea

Did you find your job at **Monster.com**?

As you may know, Monster Worldwide is the leading online recruiting and job search company in the world - a phenomenal success.

They began with simple job postings, but they had grown to offer over two dozen different products, many quite complex. Monster's corporate customers, unfortunately, mistakenly assumed they already knew all about everything Monster offered.

VP of Enterprise Marketing Janette Racicot confided to me what kept her up at night. *"I just don't know what our salespeople are saying and showing when they go out to meet with clients."*

Here's why: Monster's sales force only met with clients once or twice a year – and for only 45 minutes to an hour. How could a customer possibly absorb relevant information about two dozen products in such a short time?

Because there wasn't enough time to even explain each of the many products*, salespeople would typically guess what subset to talk about. Then they would paste together a presentation of those products.

Were they the right ones? No one knew, but those would be the only products prospects (or new managers at existing clients) would hear about.

---

* Try even listing that many offerings – any businessperson would be in a stupor before you were half-through.

The salespeople needed a way to identify what a customer was interested in, and show them the appropriate solution. The answer was to let the customer do it. We needed them to self-select.

I created a multi-tiered sales presentation that enabled customers to choose which quadrant they were most interested in. Each represented a different goal and objective — and there was enormous depth behind it — but to the customer it was simple and engaging.

The salesperson could then speak to that issue, and show only the relevant products. (All the other products remained hidden, so there was nothing to overwhelm the customer, yet they could each be instantly accessed.)

It was "Customer Directed Selling" at its best.

This new tool was presented to their sales teams[*] as well as Monster's Customer Advisory Board. It was rapidly adopted worldwide; Vice President Brian Corey credited it with helping his teams exceed sales targets even during difficult economic times.[**]

It's not enough to have information that can help a customer. Whether or not they take action depends on how it is served up.

[*] To ensure success, we brought training to each sales office, complete with small group practice sessions and coaching.

[**] Another benefit: It brought a consistent message to customers across all geographies. The EVP of Worldwide Sales called this simple solution "Phenomenal!"

The Parade of Information

Imagine we're standing on the curb awaiting a parade. There in the distance is the first of the floats; it should be here in just a minute or so.

Suddenly, zoom! That float is already here – and it's racing past us in a flash! Are they nuts – they must be going 60 miles an hour!

A split second later, zoom! The next float does the same; we can barely make out a note of the music they're playing! Then the next float and the next speed by at a too-fast pace.

This is no fun. We're leaving. Who's stupid idea was this!

Every selling situation involves some sort of parade of information. But what's the right speed?

A complex sale requires you to build. The items you bring up must build upon each other if you have any chance of creating desire.

Done right, each new point arrives just as the prospect has finished processing the previous one. That way, they're ready to focus on this new point.

To think of it visually, refer back to the 'Listen-Grasp Model' a few pages back. To build understanding, your customer has to link each bit of new information to the one they just grasped. They sort of stack on top of each other.

That stacking would look like this:

Here's the key to building understanding and desire for a complex solution. But if the timing is off, you'll get neither.

The above shows the right speed for this customer. This parade is enjoyable, worthy of their time and attention.

Why People Get Confused

The problem with that 60 mph parade was that things were coming at us too quickly. We couldn't comfortably handle them and gave up.

When selling complex or innovative solutions, salespeople often drive too fast. The intentions may be good ones – they have a lot to cover and don't want to be boring.

But, unfortunately, no one can absorb as quickly as that salesperson can talk. He or she already knows this material and has a wealth of foundation knowledge from being inside that tech company. The customer does not.

The speaker also knows what's coming next and how it all fits together. But no customer does – each will have to take time to make those connections.

As they're doing this, what happens if that salesperson keeps introducing new information? Mental mayhem.

The customer is trying to grasp it all, but when new information keeps overwhelming them, they give up.

"Hey", their brain says to them, *"Why is he interrupting me? Okay, okay, I'll try to finish absorbing the first point while holding your second one in memory.*

"Wait – what's that – another interruption?

"Now I'm getting overwhelmed. And confused. And at this pace, I'm never going to catch up. I don't like this; maybe I'll just give up and tune out. Hmm, what should I do on my vacation this year....?"

There are many ways to make it easy for the prospect to keep up with you.[*] The crucial first step is to realize that, as bright and experienced as they may be, they can't grasp nearly as fast as you can speak.

* See Chapter 6 for several effective ways to accomplish this.

The 5-Step Solution

When you need people to grasp things that are complex:

1. Call attention to the truly important points.[*]

2. Go slowly when showing complex diagrams.[**]

3. Whenever possible, use analogies from business or daily life.

4. Ask questions regularly. It keeps everyone involved and you will be able to quickly spot if they've become overwhelmed. Plus you will probably learn things that help you.

5. Summarize each section before moving to the next.

Of course, before you can apply any of these ways, you have to make sure you get and keep their attention.

* See 'Guys on Horses' in Chapter 4

** Better yet, simplify those diagrams.

Paying Attention

There's a reason we use that word: pay. We *pay* attention. Pay, as in giving of a precious or limited resource.

To effectively sell technology solutions, you need your prospects to decide to pay attention. It's the essential first step.

But we have to respect that paying attention isn't a trivial thing for a prospect to do. It requires time, thought and concentration – none of which get handed over without good reason.

Paying attention is also hard work. It is so demanding that we can't do it for do it for more than a few minutes without taking a break. It's a survival thing.

Lessons from the Wild

Think of any nature show you've ever seen. There in the open field are, say, zebras grazing. Suddenly, there's a movement in the tall grasses and everything stops. All zebra eyes shift as one to determine whether it's the wind or a hungry predator. This is smart; a hungry lion can really ruin your day. So the zebras pay attention.

The instant the zebras conclude there's no danger, they stop intensely focusing on that small area in the grasses. They relax and are now ready to pay attention elsewhere should the need arise.

Pay Attention, Then Relax

Humans don't have to worry about being attacked while dining, which is a good thing. But it's safe to say we once did. This Attention-Relaxation process is built into us. It's simply not possible to pay attention all the time. Even if a salesperson would like us to.

The timing of this Attention-Relaxation wave varies depending on the situation, but it is unavoidable. That means that every person you are speaking to will be cycling from paying attention, to relaxing, back to paying attention, then relaxing again – over and over. You just don't know when.

You know this from your own experiences when you watch others present inside your company or at conferences. Even when you want to pay careful attention, you are constantly tuning in and out.

Why They 'Just Didn't Get It'
Here's the crucial point. During those inevitable periods of relaxation, you have absolutely no control over what that person is hearing, grasping, or absorbing. None. As each audience member tunes out, even for a brief moment, they miss something.

You can build for this fact of human nature. One way is to build in time for them to take those brief breaks. They only need a few seconds.

So if a point you just made is of pivotal importance, take a moment to tell a confirming story. Or if it fits your personal style, toss in a humorous comment to provide that brief break.

Words That Work:
If you want to be certain all are on the same page, ask point blank, *"Did I properly convey just how important that is?"* If you get anything other than knowing nods, reiterate those points.

It all depends on your topic and its complexity *in the eyes of that person.*

By building for those gaps in paying attention , you control when attention can wane. You can then recapture it again after that short break. It's a great feeling of being in control – for both you and those listening to you.

You Can't Sell Me Anything

And I can't sell you anything, either.

Over the years, however, quite a few books on selling have boasted, "I can sell you anything!". They treat the prospect as an opponent – one to be conquered by the clever salesperson using tricky techniques and questions that are supposed to bully that person into taking action.

Maybe manipulative approaches work on the used car lot, but such tactics have no place in selling technology. Businesspeople have seen it all before – and they turn off immediately when they see it again.

High-integrity selling is the only approach that works in the long run. That means understanding and embracing what a salesperson can and cannot do.

All one can do is find the right people, engage them and intrigue, create desire by painting a picture of how good life will be, and then help them along.

Make it easy for them to want and buy – heroes and fortunes have been made doing just that.

Focus, Rule of Thumb

This exercise only takes 10 seconds, but it shows why prospects can fail to grasp a complete picture of your solution.

Hold your hand out in front of you, arm straight and fingers spread wide apart. Now look at your thumbnail. As you do, notice how your little finger is out of focus? In fact, so is your index finger. Now look over at your little finger so it snaps into focus. Whoa – now your thumb is fuzzy!

You never really do 'see' a complete image of your hand. That picture only comes into being when your mind stitches together all those individual parts you have focused upon.

This happens in whatever we do. When reading this sentence, for example, you absorb a word or phrase at a time. A paragraph only makes sense when your mind develops the complete thought by stitching together those small components.

That is what's going on every time you try to bring your knowledge to a customer. No matter how smart they may be, their focus is constantly shifting. It can't be prevented, but it can be overcome.

Throughout your conversations, as you delve into each facet of your solution, clearly relate it to the big picture you want them to grasp. Do this for every aspect you bring up. It may seem like overkill to you, but that's because you're so familiar with the solution you're selling. They're not.

This not only helps your contact properly grasp things, but that grasp will make it easier for them to explain it to others in their organization – and that's how a sale gains a larger audience and the momentum to become an unstoppable priority.

What Are You Really Selling?

When I speak at big sales meetings, I sometimes bring along McDonalds.

Not a bag of burgers and fries, but a perspective. Because consumer companies know something that many technology companies have trouble embracing:

Often, customers are buying something that is very different from the goods you think you are selling.

I ask the group, *"What does McDonalds sell?"* Immediately, someone will call out *"Burgers!"* Another, *"Fries!"*

This, of course is true, by the multi-millions. But then why don't we always see rows of burgers frying in their commercials? How come there's nary an oil-dripping fryer basket in sight?

So I ask the group, *"What else do they sell?"*, and the right answers soon come up. *"Convenience!" "Cleanliness!"* Bingo. They may *make* burgers and fries, but McDonalds knows their customers are buying something else.[*] That's why their commercials are all about happy people having happy times.

Every company – including yours – has such a duality.

- Rolex, for example, makes very nice watches, but any $10 quartz watch will keep time just as well. Their customers are buying luxury far more than timekeeping accuracy.

---

[*] Founder Ray Kroc: "A mother with two children in tow cares more about clean restrooms than she does about the tastiness of the burger."

- Disney World knows its customers don't fly a thousand miles to go to an amusement park – they're coming to 'The Happiest Place on Earth'.

- You know those websites that will automatically back-up your hard drive? Their marketing talks about how you could lose your precious photos forever without them, not the tech specs of their storage system.

My goal in bringing up McDonalds is to get my audience thinking about their customers' point of view.[*] That's not easy for a salesperson to do – their own company aggressively markets to them with product–centric announcements, press releases and materials. After months and years of that, seeing the customer's view requires thought and focus.

Don't make the mistake of thinking your customers are just choosing technology and services. Most likely, they see themselves buying things like confidence, safety and personal success.

Cater to those needs and desires, and you are far more likely to bring in that sale.

[*] Here's another way I do that: I take out a stack of photos and ask if they'd like to see a dozen vacation pictures of my kids. Nobody raises their hand, I continue with "Sure, but if these were photos of your kids, you'd love them." The point: Customers care about their issues, problems and needs; not yours.

Chapter 2

The New Reality
of Selling

Most sales training says all you need to do to succeed is to "listen to the customer". As you will see in this section, if you're selling technology today, that approach just isn't going to work. In many cases, it can really limit your success.

Customers may look like us and even talk like us. But in important ways – their knowledge, goals, organizational pressures and how they spend their days – they are very different.

I've already introduced you to the concept of 'Customer Vision'. In this chapter I'd like to give you a broader perspective of what factors influence how your customers think, and how to use that to increase your sales.

Let me tell you, it's an eye opener. I've lost count of all the people who have told me these concepts have forever changed the way they sell.

"Listen and Sell Benefits", RIP

You've heard "Listen and Sell Benefits" a thousand times. It's part of every sales training course, probably because it's both generic and it worked, up until a few years ago.

Today, it's just plain wrong.

"Listen & Sell Benefits" is dead. The internet killed it. L&SB hinged on you being able to listen to the right level people, so you could sell the benefits that decision makers cared about.

That was back in the day when customers needed to meet with salespeople to learn about new things. Those meetings led to relationships. Only with that relationship will L&SB work.

Today, salespeople arrive after the movie has started. Customers now check the web first, which changes everything.

Often the person who has time to talk with you is way down in the pecking order. He or she wants very specific answers to their already-determined criteria. Listen only to them and you're limiting your chances for success.

Listening is only the start. Selling technology today means finding out the real motivations, and often finding the right executives.[*] That's why this book is filled with ideas and specific approaches that will bring you immediate advantages over anyone who is still counting on L&SB to deliver like it did decades ago, in simpler times.

---

[*] See 'Selling Senior Executives' in Chapter 4 for ways their priorities fundamentally differ from those who report to them.

The Harsh Truth About 'Pains'

"Find their pains." "Well, I determine their pains."
"We just need to find their pains and remove those pains."

Pains, pains, pains. If there is one buzzword that sales training jargon has given us over the past 20 years, it is *"pains"*.

Pains are no longer nearly as relevant as they once were. Most big pains have been fixed – but customers don't know what's *possible*.

Nowadays, most technology solutions are about taking a company to new heights – not about addressing annoying pains they well know but haven't been able to fix.[*]

Pain-oriented selling had its day, but looking back it was a bit like picking the low fruit. Prospects knew their pains; so did their upper management. They were relatively easy to probe for – and once found, selling one's solution was a straightforward process.

Today, however, known-yet-unsolved pains are much rarer. Your solution probably can take a customer to new heights – but that, compared to a pain reliever, requires different skills to sell.

Interestingly, it's often the larger tech companies – who institutionalized pain-selling training a few years ago – whose salespeople are still talking about pains and looking for them. Smaller companies can adapt more quickly as customers change.

Flexible Business Systems is a services company on Long Island, NY. One of their divisions brings managed services and enhanced web

[*] But, as Tom Millea, who manages teams at Novell, points out, removing known pain is removing operational expense, which is still a legitimate IT objective.

presence to small and medium size businesses. A likely prospect for them might be a company where the office manager has been handling update patches for all the PCs, buying Google AdWords, and taking care of their data backup with an online company.

And if you asked that office manager, there are no pains.

At least none they know of. In fact, they're pretty proud of things; that office manager sees his or her value in part reflected by doing those updates and calling a tech repair company when problems occur. Trying to sell to them based on pains is a losing proposition.

Flexible has figured out the better way to sell such pain-free prospects Is to address the *dreams* of that business.

- *The dream* of more customers and revenue by showing how they could improve their web presence beyond using AdWords.

- *The dream* of accomplishing more with those servers and PCs, as opposed to being stuck in the past and merely maintaining the way they've been doing things for years.

- *The dream* of never having technology failures interrupt their business – of being up and running literally the next day even after a server crashes.

At companies of all sizes, dreams motivate executives. Heroes are made when dreams are achieved – dreams of growth, of seizing new opportunities.

As we'll see in a moment, that's why dreams are so powerful in selling today – far more so than hoping to find still-existing pains.

In today's business world, dreams of greater success – not pains -- are what drive priorities, attention and tech spending.

The Power of Dreams

At each of your target accounts, your power is in making dreams come true.

Think about the technologies we all now use every day:

- It wasn't a pain that flat screen TVs addressed; no one was lamenting how their old TV was too big to hang on the wall. No, they fulfilled a dream – much bigger picture, yet taking up less space.

- The iPod wasn't created because people were in pain about Walkmen or CD players, which were already quite compact. The dream, however, was something so tiny you could have all your music with you everywhere.

- No one was complaining about the pain of using a pay phone – the dream was a phone you could have with you anywhere.

When selling to business, dreams appeal to executives' desires to reach new heights. The person who shows them what is now possible can help them in important ways – and may even change the future of that entire enterprise.

That's why the top achiever speaks to dreams – as they make those possibilities come alive to the prospect, they will sell circles around competitors still expecting a pain-filled, pain-knowing world.

The Better Mousetrap Company is Out of Business

"Our product is so far ahead, it really should sell itself."

I often meet product people who can't imagine anyone not wanting their new creation. *"You know, 'Build a better mousetrap and the world will beat a path to your door'? Well this is that better mousetrap."*

Maybe so. But in our busy, fast-paced world:

1. No one knows that you've built it.

2. Even if you tell them, few will invest the time to learn why you claim it's better.

3. The ones who do won't necessarily agree it's better, or that much better.

4. Of those who agree, few will see good reason to mention it to the people in their company with money to spend on mousetraps.

5. And even if they do, what will they answer when those people say to just wait until next quarter, or until all the mousetraps we already have are used up?

As the world has learned countless times, you can go broke waiting for the world to beat a path to your door. Creating is just the first step. The company's fortunes and future depend on *selling*.

If people in your company believe that your new technology will sell itself, tell them this: If it does, it will be the first one in history to do so.

No Budget Doesn't Have to Mean No Sale

If your refrigerator broke down tomorrow, what would you do?

One option would be to check if you have allotted funds in your yearly budget plan to fix it – and if you haven't, to do without a refrigerator until next year's budget kicks in. Right.

No, instead you would find the money right away. Because having a refrigerator is a priority to you. So you'll find the money by not spending in some other area.

That's why you shouldn't assume a sale is impossible just because your initial contact cites 'no budget'. Every day, companies are buying things that were not envisioned back last year when budgets were decided.[*]

That's one of the reasons why senior executives exist – to find money for new priorities that have arisen since the budget was planned last year. They do it when strategic or competitive pressures dictate needs or create opportunities.

If your technology can bring that company a significant advantage, find the person who cares about that advantage and has the power to move money around to get it.

---

[*] Analogies like this one, outside of that customer's particular business, can be very useful. Served up at the right moment, they can open minds.

Same Planet, Different Worlds

In many ways you and your customers are alike. You're both humans with the driving needs and wants that all humans share. You both may be sharp, hardworking, high integrity, caring and kind.

But when we look at day-to-day life – and especially concerning the solution you're selling – you may be worlds apart.

	You	Customer
Interest in Your Product	High	Less – Varies
Foundation Knowledge	High	Less – Varies
Desire to Focus on Details	High	Less – Zero?
Knowledge of Internal Issues	Low	High
Distractions Right Now	None	Many
Will Get Bored or Confused	No	Good chance

It's only natural to assume that customers are quite similar to you. But as you can see from this chart, they're not.

What's the impact of these fundamental differences? Think twice before assuming that your prospect will respond to the same things, and in the same ways, that you would.

In most cases, you have to sell to them very differently than *you* would want to be sold to if you were in their seat.

The End Or the Beginning?

Here's another way customers and salespeople see things differently: To the salesperson, the big moment is when the customer signs. That's when the sale is closed and you begin focusing on the next opportunity.

But to the customer, your big moment closing the deal was really the *beginning* of this relationship.

Now their work really begins – they have all sorts of unknowns ahead. They include bringing in your solution, living with those changes, and handling whatever problems and personal risks for them that might arise.

That's a big difference, and the best salespeople understand this.[*] They stay close and continue to give attention after the signing takes place. It is just what the customer wants – and often leads to more business.

---

[*] They even talk about this during the sale, so the customer knows they can expect the good care and attention to continue later on.

When Mentoring Vanished

If you're wondering why customers can act so strangely, here's the reason. About 15 years ago, mentoring disappeared. You feel the impact in your selling every day.

Mentoring was the business version of what the trades call apprenticeship. Younger people in a corporation learned best practices from those with more experience. It was how each new generation learned the smartest approaches as well as mistakes to avoid.

It vanished quietly during the internet boom times in the late 1990s. Back then, the media would spotlight each week's latest 22 year old zillionaire and tell us yet again how youth obviously knew everything. That meant the notion of older folks teaching them was clearly obsolete.

Mentoring is coming back now, but the result is that there is a generation of un-mentored businesspeople out there. And you're selling to them.

That doesn't make them bad, but it sure does make them varied. This makes selling to them tougher and far less predictable. Many are hungry for gentle guidance.*

The best technology salespeople know that their job requires they act as a knowledgeable guide, not merely as a helpful assistant.

---

* As detailed in later chapters, a very useful phrase is, "The way we typically do this is..." It tells them that there's a right way to do things, one that other companies have followed. Even if they insist they want something different, this is helpful and reassuring for them to know.

What's the Competition Saying?

I'm frequently brought in to companies because they want to improve their win rates over competitors.

One of the first questions I ask is, *"What are your customers hearing from your competitors?"*

Often the answer is that no one really knows. Years ago, that may have been understandable, since you, of course, can't sit in on those meetings.

These days, however, you don't need that seat. Competitors will gladly tell you, if you know where to look. If your business has a few key competitors, you can consider their websites as treasure troves. Get in the habit of spending 10 or 15 minutes every few weeks clicking around over there. Here's how you will benefit:

1. You'll Spot Important Changes:
One benefit of frequent checking is that you'll know when they change their message. Home page changes don't happen without multiple levels of management being involved. From those changes, you are getting insight into their business strategy and what they're discussing with prospects.

Have they changed their focus from departmental sales to enterprise? What does their new demo highlight? Are they trying to position themselves as thought leaders?

2. You Can Check Their Reference Stories
The stories on their site are probably the ones they're telling to customers on sales calls. This is very useful to know; you can now tailor your selling to minimize their claimed advantages and underscore yours. Then look deeper.

You just may find that they still have a 'success story' up there from a company who has since switched to you. It happens, and what a great story you now have until they notice.[*]

Compare their reference stories with yours. How well written are they? How easy to find? If the ones on your site are not as compelling, have the problem fixed.

---

3. You Can Check Their White Papers and Reports

Are there any new ones? If there are, chances are good their sales team is using them with customers. It's amazing how many companies will simply allow you to download their presentations – and how easy it is to adjust your own sales story around the key areas they highlight.

4. Look for Press Releases, Management Changes, Executive Blogs and Tweeting

These areas can provide a wealth of information for you; all you have to do is look.

The first step to outselling a competitor is knowing what they're saying and doing. Even if your marketing team is doing this sort of research, you can't go wrong by investing a few minutes every week or two.

Often the little things can sway a sale, and there's no upside in being unaware of what key competitors are telling the world.

---

[*] Why is it still up there? Their marketing folks are overworked. Putting new items up is a priority and everyone notices. Removing old ones? Not nearly as important.

Decide Emotionally, Justify Logically

That's what we humans do.

In every facet of life, whether choosing a house or a spouse, emotions are big part of the equation. At the office, however, we deny their influence. How many times have you heard a customer say,

"If you want to sell to us, just show us a superior solution!"[*]

Emotions, however, are not a choice. They come as standard equipment and are present any time humans are involved. Even when the decision is about cold, hard technology.

We may want to believe that choices are made on specs and 'facts', but they're not. Whenever choices are made by humans, emotions come into play.

They include big factors such as liking you, trusting you and believing you care about their success (and not just making your sale).

In any important selling situation, it's a good idea to ask yourself: What possible emotions are involved here, and what can I do to address those factors so they help me?

---

[*] Really? Try selling that person a superior solution that just happens to make his job superfluous and let me know how it goes.

Customers Always Act Sensibly and Predictably*

*From their point of view, that is.

What may seem surprising, erratic, or downright lunacy to you makes complete sense to them. This can be because of their fears, lack of understanding, or assumptions. The better you get at 'Customer Vision' – seeing things from their perspective – the more powerful you become.

Follow the Money

ATG had a problem. Their remarkable web technology brought a uniquely customized experience to web shoppers and was already being used by hundreds of leading online retailers.

But despite this, Worldwide SVP of Sales Greg Lazar explained to me that sales cycles had been growing longer.

That shouldn't have been the case. Their solution, among other benefits, increases online sales revenue because fewer shoppers abandon their shopping carts before paying. But inexplicably, ATG was finding it harder to generate interest and good meetings.[*]

They had the right solutions – but were they talking to the right people?

My research found that their salespeople were typically calling on people in the department responsible for running the site. They had sold this way for years; it was their 'comfort zone'.

That problem was that many of those people didn't think they had a problem. No pains here; those technical folks were proud of their well-running site.

We needed to find the people with dreams. It was time for ATG to change how they sold.

As an immediate first step, we added an approach to directly approach the VP or SVP of Merchandising at those target accounts. These are the people with dreams of higher sales revenue each day – they would see the value in reducing abandoned shopping carts.

---

[*] ATG had even tried approaches such as having meetings set up for them by an outside firm, but results were disappointing. I've found that's often the case.

Reducing the abandonment rate by even a small amount can easily increase sales by millions of dollars a year. This is what makes heroes.

We then brought a workshop to ATG's salespeople that took them into the mind of those executives and what it takes to sell to them.

It included <u>Words That Work</u> for their specific sale, and practice in no-pressure small groups so each salesperson could adapt the approaches to their own style.[*] It was piloted first in North America, then brought to Europe, Asia and Australia.

With this training and new tools, soon ATG's salespeople were meeting with those business executives, and the meetings were focused on their sales-revenue dreams, not on technical capabilities.

The approach worked quickly, with a remarkable ROI. As Greg Lazar put it, our work was *"instrumental in winning more than 120 new accounts."*

The person who is responsible for a technology area isn't necessarily the only one in that corporation who cares about it.

Sure, IT was still an important part of making the sale eventually happen. But the lesson here is that, at any target company, there may be more than one person or department that is worthy of your attention.

---

[*] Without this, there's no comfort and no proficiency. And without that, there's no confidence. Know anybody who would want to practice – and risk looking foolish – in front of real customers?

Customers Know Less

That's why they're meeting with you.

If they already had vast knowledge about this possible purchase, they'd be done already. The purchase would have been made and they'd be on to other things.

Right now they are trying to figure out your business, their choices, and what makes best sense for them. So they're investigating, exploring, and talking with you. It's what people do when they don't yet know enough to take action.

Don't assume the people you talk with know nearly as much as you do. Even brilliant people who nod non-stop can know shockingly little about what makes your company and solution so valuable.

Customers Know More

In one way, customers today know far more than they ever did in the past. That's because they've done some web exploring before meeting with you.

Which areas? What competitors? How deeply?

It's impossible to know. The best approach is to have them guide you. Ask outright:

Words That Work:
"Most of the people we meet with have already explored the web to get some background knowledge. Can I ask the sort of research you've done, and what questions or areas are most important to you?"

Then listen carefully[*]; you will get useful information about this person and how they view the purchase.

Feel free to ask follow-on questions about their familiarity with specific technologies and competitors. This is also the perfect time to ask if others in their company are also doing research into this.[**]

---

[*] It's tempting to jump in as soon as they mention something about which you have great information. Resist. Instead, let them go on and jot down the many points they mention.

[**] You will want to get them involved; see 'Who Must Be in This Boat?' in Chapter 3.

15 Things I Know About Your Customer*

1. They have dreams.

2. Their business succeeds by creating customers and selling things, not by spending money on technology.

3. They can't absorb as fast as you can explain.

4. They see risks in places you do not.

5. They don't want this purchase to ever haunt them.

6. They will not buy what they cannot explain to others.

7. They need to be able to justify the purchase in two sentences.

8. They're very, very busy right now.

9. They want it to be easy.

10. They have insecurities they won't mention.

11. They've never bought this exact type of solution at this point in time.

12. There's a lot they don't know.

13. They get distracted.

14. They need others in the boat for it to sail.

15. They see you differently than you see you.

* This is a good list to review before each sales call.

Love To Buy, Hate To Be Sold

"So Ken, should I stop by to pick up the order Tuesday, or would Thursday be more convenient?"

It was years ago, back I was a buyer at Macy's in New York. That salesman was trying the 'Alternate-Choice Close' on me. He had been trying other slick techniques; he must have thought he was so clever.[*]

What he didn't realize is that no one likes 'being sold'
Buying is about *having power*. That's why people love to buy.

When we buy, we are exerting our power. It feels good, and It almost doesn't matter how much money is involved.

Even if it's just a cheap yard sale item or choosing which restaurant to go to, you are master of your realm, using the power that is uniquely yours.

In business, the buying may be for an expensive solution that determines the company's competitiveness and future. That's a lot of power. To your customer, it is a great feeling as they wield that power wisely to gain the benefits and possible accolades of their good judgment.

But when a salesperson tries pressure tactics, it is an attempt to rob them of that power. No one likes that; nor do we like that person.

The smart salesperson is here to create desire. They're not trying to 'sell' – on the contrary, they're trying to make easy and enjoyable to buy.

---

* You're correct – I did no business with him.

55

How Do Humans Buy Technology?

Nervously. Cautiously. Inconsistently. There are almost as many ways to judge and buy tech solutions as there are prospects.

No one went to school for this. Even if they did, it wouldn't matter. Technology advances and transforms so fast that what might have made great sense five years ago is absolutely wrong today.[*]

There are so many unknowns to consider. Technology solutions are usually expensive, with high-visibility impact on people (and possibly the entire organization). You don't really know how it will work out until after it's all bought and making that impact.

 Add all that together and it can be a bit scary.

That's why salespeople are so crucial to success. It's their job to size up a situation, decide the best way to stand out as uniquely desirable, and bring confidence to an overwhelmed prospect.

As you work your magic, never forget that even the most confident-appearing prospect knows there are many things they do not know. Use this fact to bring value – and comfort – at every interaction.

---

[*] It was only a few years ago that colleges were proud their new lecture halls had Ethernet wiring at every seat.

9 Things Every Customer Wants*

Pretty much, they want what you want in life.

1. They want to look smart.

2. They want to avoid needless risks.

3. They want to feel important.

4. They want to succeed, however they define that.

5. They want to get home on time to enjoy life.

6. They want to somehow get ahead of all the work and priorities that keep piling up.

7. They want to avoid looking foolish.

8. They want to avoid being vulnerable.

9. They want to be a hero.

Figure out how your solution gets them what they want.

* This is a good list to review before each sales call.

Who Is the Competition?

These days, it's not only the usual suspects. It's much bigger and more complicated than that.

Suppose I come into your new car dealership. You sell Fords, and I tell you I'm thinking about getting your latest mid-size sedan. Who's your competition?

Other new car dealers, sure. Other Ford dealers? Right again. But that's not where the list stops. There's no law that says I have to buy a new car. For the same amount of money, I might also be considering a used Lexus. Or I could keep my old car and use the money to go on vacation. So, in a sense, you're also competing against Hawaii.

The same is taking place at most accounts you're trying to sell.

In a fast changing world, your competition includes everything else they could be spending this money on – including new priorities that may arise tomorrow.

That's why your benefits must be big and compelling. If they're not, those dollars you are counting on may suddenly get shifted and your sale may vanish.

Chapter 3

It's Called the Sales Process

You've been around, you've taken your fair share of sales training. So you know selling is a clear, predictable, precise step-by-step process, complete with unmistakable milestones.

Are you laughing already?

It's so much more complicated in our business. Technology solutions don't get bought unless many people and departments act in concert – it's no wonder the process has starts and stops, detours and dead-ends.

The key is to look at the process from the customer's point of view. In this section, you will find proven ways to keep that process on track.

Stuck On the Sales Ladder

You know the 'Sales Ladder'. Every company has one – it's the diagram that shows the steps you'd like every prospect to quickly follow. (Your version may be a horizontal one, with boxes instead of rungs).

The notion is simple: Prospects or suspects start at the bottom and (hopefully) advance up the rungs to the top, at which point you've made the sale. Such a model can have value inside one's company; for example, so all new hires will grasp the steps to bring in the sale.

Prospects, however, couldn't care less.

Why should they? Those steps or boxes are about what *you* want them to do, not what *they* want to do. Plus, each of your competitors also has a similar ladder for them to climb. Obviously, they won't be proceeding to the top of all those ladders.

Here's the key to having more prospects make it to the top of yours: It's all about the rungs.

How Many Rungs Should a Ladder Have?
Suppose I asked you to help me fix some loose shingles on my roof. I bring out my ladder and you start climbing, but then after a few steps, you notice the next rung is pretty far away. To you, that makes it too risky to proceed. So you stop where you are.

I may tell you to keep going, but despite the fact I'd like you to advance, you won't be moving ahead.

Look at your sales process as a customer might – are there missing rungs? To put it another way, can you get more prospects to

---

proceed on up to the top if you provide extra steps for the cautious ones?

A small step is better than no advance at all. You might want to offer prospects more than one choice at a particular spot. For example:

<u>Words That Work:</u>
 "At this point, we can either get a data sample to plug in and show the impact, or we could instead expand our discussion to include (executive) before doing that. You know your organization best; what's the right step to take?"

From your contact's answer, you now know whether it takes an extra rung in order to keep them moving up your ladder.

Prospects will always see risk very differently than your company does. By being attuned to this, you can make it easy and safe for them to keep on climbing.

How to Read Your Prospect's Mind

Every salesperson I meet wants some sort of advantage over the competition. Here's a big one – knowing what your customers are thinking.

No crystal ball is necessary. We live in a fast-paced business world where your prospects are steered by industry trends, competitor's moves, and current hot-topics. The minds you want to read are all being influenced by industry magazines, conferences and trade shows, plus, of course, websites and maybe blogs. (If your contact isn't directly influenced by these forces, then the executives who decide their priorities certainly are.)

It's this total picture that determines what they care about and how they act. Here are ways to know more about the issues that are shaping their priorities, even if they won't confide in you.

Discovering Industry Trends:
Want to find out, for sure, the current topics and trends their executives are thinking about?

1. Do a web search for upcoming conferences in their field.

2. Keep clicking until you find the agendas for those conferences.

3. Now dive into the descriptions of those sessions. You've just found out what topics the leaders in their industry consider of paramount importance.[*]

How to use this information? First figure out ways it applies to what you're selling. Then work those topics into your conversations (or

---

[*] You might also want to do a search on the speakers; you're likely to find a blog or other information that will add greatly to your grasp of this topic.

----

your phone messages) as you reach out to engage prospects and existing customers.[*]

Leveraging Their Trade Magazines:
Every industry has its own trade journals; they show up every month on the desks of the people you want to influence. If you work with a particular industry, you should subscribe to a few of them (many are free).

You should also browse the websites of those magazines:

- Check out the forums and discussion groups

- Browse the online edition of the latest issue

- Explore the archives to get a sense of history or trends

Do this and customers will find you incredibly knowledgeable and focused on their industry – especially when compared to competing salespeople who haven't put in this effort.

---

[*] This knowledge is particularly useful when trying to reach higher levels of management.

People Buy From People They Like

This is one of the simplest and oldest rules of selling, but also one of the most important.

It's true even for the most technical purchase. In fact, the more important and expensive the purchase, the more influential that personal respect and liking becomes.

So let your personality and good nature come through even as you delve into all those features and specifics. Let them know you as a person. *

But what if you're not the most personable or outgoing individual?

It doesn't matter, as long as you truly care about helping your customer succeed. People can sense this. You know the old adage: "People don't care what you know – until they know that you care."

These factors may not show up on any spec sheet or competitive analysis, but they are some of your most influential selling tools. A unique benefit of doing business with you is doing business with *you*.

---

* See 'Introducing…You!' in Chapter 6 for a way to do this that only takes 30 seconds.

Goals vs. Non-Goals

Meetings cost time and money. To be worth either, you should have a goal for each meeting and a way to measure if you've reached it.

I am always surprised how few companies have taught their sales team the notion of Goals vs. Non-Goals. Non-goals are merely activities; one could perform them yet not be any closer to bringing in new business. A real goal is measurable – it is an action that takes you closer to the sale.

Non-Goals:
- To show up and give our presentation

- To explain the great new product or org chart

- To ask about their pains and plans

- To stay in touch and give them an update

- To explain as much as I can and answer all their questions

Real Goals:
- To get a sample of their data

- To have them expand the audience to include...

- To determine a schedule for ...

- To have them arrange for me to meet their boss

- To have them introduce us to other divisions

Before every interaction, ask yourself: What is my goal, and how will I know if I've reached it?

The Annual Report Mistake

"To find out about a company and what's important over there, check out their annual report."

Not anymore.

Years ago, when public information was rare and hard to find, those annual reports were all you had. Even then, while *you* may have scoured that annual report, it often turned out that very few of the people you called upon at that company knew what was in it.

Today the annual report can't keep up with the pace of business. In the months since it was written, much has changed. It still may look very official, but what you're reading may no longer be in the plan.

Fortunately, there are now additional – and better – ways to get a read on a target account.[*]

Start with Their Press Releases: They are much more timely than the annual report – and they're very easy to find on their website.

You will read about a new senior VP taking over a division – and you can be sure he or she is there to make changes. Did they just acquire a company? That means assimilation, investing in new markets, and people who want it all to be a success. You get the idea; there can be gold in those press releases.

Use Social Media: LinkedIn, for example, will let you do some fascinating data mining. Do a search on the company, and you now have a list of all sorts of people who work there.

[*] Also see 'How to Read Your Prospect's Mind'

Click around to see who recently joined the company. You will learn about executives who are below 'press release importance', but might be important to you.

Any division or department with a new leader is an opportunity – how can your solution help that person achieve their dream of succeeding in that new job?

Check News on Their Competitors: If one of them is, say, acquiring a distributor or entering a new market, odds are good that they too are exploring such matters. You may be able to get in early.

Read Their Industry Journals: As mentioned earlier in this chapter, you'll learn about trends or upcoming regulations that can show you where new opportunities lie. Plus you sure will have credibility in meetings compared to competitors who know less about their world.

No matter how well done, research has its limitations. It may hint at what that company should care about, but won't take care of engaging and intriguing those key individuals. That's your job.

Fatal Assumptions*

The sales process can be derailed with just one bad meeting or customer interaction. I've found these are almost always based on false assumptions. Here are some of the most common ones:

- They know almost as much as I do.

- They understand my value.

- They interpret phrases and acronyms exactly as I do.

- They'd love a demo right now.

- They'll read what I give them.

- They'll remember and tell others.

- Sending them my complete, detailed slideshow will have them showing it to others and lead to new meetings.

- They know how to influence others.

- They'll champion this because it's as important to them as it is to me.

- This sale is moving along.

If you find yourself thinking or saying any of these fatal assumptions, it's time for you to use your 'Customer Vision'.

* This is a good list to review before each sales call.

A Lesson from Car Dealers

No, I'm not suggesting you sell like a car salesman: *"Buddy, what would it take for me to put you behind the wheel today of this turbo-charged beauty complete with the ultra-luxury package and our special triple-double-undercoating?"*

But here's a lesson from that industry about using the customer's imagination. It happened when I was shopping for my first luxury car. The salesman was soft-spoken and professional. At just the right moment, he said, in a friendly way,

"Ken, can you imagine how this will look in your driveway? How it will look when you drive up to your friends' houses?"

It was brilliant. He, of course, had no idea what my driveway looked like. But I did. There I was, picturing this car in it. That salesperson had me envisioning life once I owned that car. Smart, very smart.

People in business have imaginations, too.

Words That Work:
At the right moment, what happens if you say, *"Imagine how executives will feel when all this information is easy for people to find and use. When there are no more problems, no more reinventing the wheel each time because…"*

Your contacts will fill in the blanks. They know who those executives are, they know what their offices look like. They can see themselves getting congratulated for this project's benefits.

Don't mistake this for manipulation – it's not. On the contrary, you are helping them imagine what your solution will bring to that company and to them.

Your Words Evaporate

So do mine. The spoken word vanishes like a wisp of smoke the instant it leaves your lips. Unlike you reading this book, your prospect has no way to go back to review anything you said or to confirm they remembered it correctly.

On any sales call, you utter thousands of words. Not a person on earth could remember them all. Yet what your prospect remembers and repeats will determine if this sale moves forward and at what pace.

Much is new to your prospect, and technology solutions are complex. Don't assume he or she will remember your key points well enough to confidently mention them to others. Most of the time, they can't and won't. Even worse is when they remember things incorrectly. You can you lose out without ever never knowing what happened.

Think: How can I make this tangible? Figure out what you can leave behind that helps them do that. Not some glossy brochure; what's better is a brief and personal refresher about your meeting.

Resist taking the easy path: *"I'll send you my slides."*[*] Busy people rarely will open the file, and ever more rarely will take the time to slog through each slide and distill it down to something useful to them. Would you?[**]

[*] Also resist telling them, "You can find it all on our website.", expecting they will find the time and desire to go exploring. Make it easy for them.

[**] Want to guess the chances of them forwarding it to others and those people taking the time to open it and begin slogging?

71

Instead, you do that distilling for them. Send an email with the subject line: '3 Slide Summary of Today's Meeting' – they're likely to open it.

If they like what they see – if it's concise and useful – they may forward it on to others and help sell for you. Creating this tangible tool that lives on after your words are long gone is a very leveraged use of your time.[*]

The best tangible-tool is often the one you create during that meeting. It is impressive if you create a diagram based on what they just told you about their infrastructure and needs. And they now have it and can use it to explain things to others.

In a small meeting, you can create this on a sheet of plain paper. If your meeting is in a conference room, use the easel if you can, instead of the sure-to-be-erased whiteboard.

[*] See 'PowerPoint – Friend or Foe?' in Chapter 6 for a money-making skill I'd like you to acquire.

Phone Calls Evaporate, Too

More and more, pivotal meetings are taking place from afar, either via web meetings, video conferences, or simply over the phone.

In those cases it's even more urgent that you bring some permanence – a virtual interaction is weaker to begin with than an in-person one.

Send an email with that tangible tool. Ideally, do it the same day as the call, while it is still fresh in their mind. Mention that you will be doing this as you close your conversation, then do it shortly thereafter.

This simple action speaks volumes about your level of follow-through.

"We Lost on Price. Again."

Don't be so sure about that. It may not be the case, even if they told you, point blank, *"We chose someone else because of price."*

When you hear that, it's tempting to blame your company's pricing for your lost sale. But what else was that customer going to say?

It's like when a job seeker doesn't get the job and asks for feedback. Suppose you want to be helpful and say, *"Well, you showed up late, knew little about our company, and the only questions you asked were about vacation time and if you could leave early on Tuesdays."*

Think you'd get heartfelt appreciation for your candor? No chance – instead you may get a lawsuit. That's why interviewers have learned to say, *"Many qualified candidates, but we could only hire one."*

For the same reasons, prospects say, *"Sorry, it was price."* This purchase is behind them now. Price is the easiest reason to give.

Oh, it certainly is possible that your pricing is not competitive. But don't jump to that conclusion just because that's what a prospect tells you so they can politely get off the phone and back to work.

It may have been because they didn't grasp your benefits or what they were getting for their money. Maybe your contact was weak. Or they never really intended to switch from their current vendor. Or anything in between.

Hey, it could even have been that you were outsold by a competing salesperson who did more research and had better follow-through.[*]

----

[*] What? You didn't want to hear that? Ok, it was price.

Don't Let Them Look Stupid

Want to know why many technology sales go nowhere after the first meeting? People in hierarchies don't want to look foolish in the eyes of their boss.

Each of your prospects has learned what happens when they tell their manager about an intriguing meeting they had with a salesperson. The boss asks a question or two. If they can't intelligently answer those questions, they look unprepared and unprofessional. They thought they'd be showing their value – instead, just the opposite happened.

If I'm your prospect and I even *think* there's a chance of looking foolish, I'll take the safe route and not mention the topic at all. Problem solved.

You can use this fact of human nature to your advantage. Done right, it makes you even more valuable to your contact.

Let's say you've just had a good meeting where you explained your solution and why management will appreciate learning about it. If you want your contact to feel confident bringing this topic up with his or her manager, follow with:

Words That Work:
"As you know, we work with many companies. Based on my experience, when you bring this up to others there are three questions you can expect your manager (or that division head) will likely ask."

My next sentence would be this: *"Should I quickly go over them?"*
The prospect's reaction will tell me volumes about where his or her

----

head is at regarding this purchase. If there's any reluctance, as if to say this won't be necessary, I know not to expect much here.

More likely, they will be curious. So tell them the questions to expect, along with succinct answers those executives will find valuable.

Words That Work:
After that discussion, help them further by suggesting:

"Would it be helpful if I send you a brief email that has these questions and answers in it?"

Then get that out to them that same day, so they can chat up your solution while it is still fresh in their mind.

This is really a crucial part of your selling to that prospect. You're helping them envision good outcomes if they bring this up to others. Not only are you bringing them confidence, but you're also underscoring your value in making them a hero.

Repeat Performances, Avoiding

"This was very valuable – I'd like to get you back to show this to other people around here."

If what they mean is they'd like you to come back and do it again for a peer or two of theirs, I have a suggestion: Don't.

While their intentions may be fine, this could be a recipe for lengthening your sales cycle. That repeat performance brings you no closer to the businesspeople who can say, *"Wow – we need this as soon as possible!"* and the money they can find to make that happen.

Contacts can forget that your time has value and you must pass on other opportunities in order to bring a repeat performance to them. In situations like this, instead of meekly agreeing, say:

Words That Work:
"Bill, I'm glad you see the value here and want to expose more people to it. Can I ask that we expand the meeting to also include business managers of some key areas that can benefit from this?

"For example, I can show … and then suggest specific examples and the departments to which they will appeal.

"That's how we typically do it; at other customers such as …, …, and …, doing this was appreciated by all."

This is said, of course, with a smile in your voice. It accomplishes quite a bit in less than a minute.

1. It conveys that you appreciate his reaction.

2. It introduces the idea of expanding the meeting to include business types. This may not have even occurred to him.

3. It gently says that he will be appreciated by those business people for doing that.

4. It establishes that it's not common for you to return without an expanded audience.

5. It mentions three customers who did this and it worked out well for all.

What if Bill balks? It depends. The way you phrased it, you kept your options open. If the account is worth it and there's no other way, you might decide to go back just to meet with his peers.

If you do agree to that, you have every right to ask:

Words That Work:
"But can I ask, if we do that this time, that our next meeting will include business people?"

Alternatively, if you feel the account isn't worth a repeat, try this:

Words That Work:
"Bill, I wish I could. At my company though, my manager is against 'unexpanded second meetings'. Any chance we can get at least one business manager or your manager involved?"

Bill's answer will tell you a lot. Now you can make an intelligent choice on how to best invest your time.

Who Must Be In This Boat?

"Yeah, sorry. It turns out that we can't move ahead without..."

Recognize this? It's the sound of a sale falling apart. It usually happens because your contact hadn't thought about, or didn't anticipate, who needed to be involved for this sale to happen.

Now that they've checked, it turns out that final sign-off by the VP is also needed. This boat won't be leaving the dock unless he or she is aboard.

The worst time to find this out is when it's too late. You get a slightly embarrassed call, some mumbling about changes in priorities and a new executive focus, and then the bombshell hits: That needed signature won't be coming; the sale is off.

The best time for this discovery is early on. That still affords you time to build your sale so it includes all the right players.

How can you avoid this problem?

You Have to Ask
Don't be shy. Even if your contact acts as if he or she controls everything, you have every right to ask how things work over there. After all, you're investing your time and your company's resources.

At the very first meeting, ask:

<u>Words That Work:</u>
"Lee, help me understand how things work at your company. At some of our accounts, all it takes is sign off from a manager to make this happen. At others, it requires all sorts of levels of management getting involved at different times.

"If this purchase is to take place, who needs to be involved, and at what stage do you think they would get brought in?"

You Have to Listen Carefully
He or she is about to tell you the likelihood of your sale happening. For example, you may hear that they expect a long cycle where the real powers aren't involved until late. Until then your sale is uncertain, which is not a good thing.

You Have to Guide Them
You might suggest a path slightly different from the slow uncertain one they've just suggested.

Words That Work:
"At most of our customers, it made sense to get that top executive involved early on, just for an overview meeting.

"That way, we learn how they feel and what matters most to them. It can save a lot of time and wasted effort. Can that happen here?"

You may or may not get the answer you're hoping for. But at least you now know the lay of the land over there and can invest your time wisely.

There's a temptation to avoid such questions, hoping that this will be the easy fast sale you've been dreaming of. Resist that temptation. My experience has been that speedy sales never happen unless all the right people are in the boat early on.

"The Committee Will Decide"

The era of the lone-wolf decision maker is over, at least for a while. These days it's all about consensus. There's safety in numbers.

This doesn't make life easier for the technology salesperson. The committee will decide – but it's unlikely you will get to meet with them as a group. You will be notified of the outcome, thank you. [*]

The problem here is that your contact, who may be brilliant in many ways, may not be masterful in group dynamics or in presenting to a group. Unless you take initiative, you can easily lose out just because a competitor's contact was more knowledgeable about such things.

Here's what we did for a client of mine, **Gyrus Systems**, when they were facing this problem. Their president Bob Dust was fed up with losing because of closed-door committees and wanted an approach all his salespeople could use. We came up with one that began producing literally within its first week in use. It was built on three components:

1. Gently Teach Your Contacts How to Have an Impact
Gyrus' salespeople were taught how to prepare their contacts for what would happen in the committee.

Words That Work:
 "At other companies, what we've found is that when the committee examines this, they will appreciate learning about ... and ...."

Many technical evaluators are so caught up in their work that they don't think about where it is all leading. Nose to the tree, they can't

---

[*] See 'We Lost on Price. Again.' for why you may never get the full story.

see the forest. This step now had that person thinking about that meeting.

You can start by asking how things will work. Very often your contact will only have loose ideas of what to expect. That lets you ask more and at least speak to possibilities. What you are doing is getting that contact thinking about how they will influence the committee in that meeting. This is good.

2. Create Self-Motivation to Make a Strong Case
Remember, this is all new to this company. These people have never debated these competing solutions at this point in time. There are no best practices they can use, unless you enlighten them how to handle specific situations.

Get specific. You probably know who the other contenders are, so teach your contact.

Words That Work:
 "You can be pretty sure that the person in charge of (competitor) has been told about (key advantage they claim). What will likely be most important to upper managers and help the company, however, is how we..."

Naturally, a lot depends on your relationship with your contact, as well as his or her personality and experience. One way or another, you want your contact to appreciate how it is a good reflection on them if they make an effective case.

3. Give Them the Ammunition They Will Need
Think about that actual committee meeting. What will your contact bring?

This can mean the difference between winning or losing. In a committee meeting, opinions can form quickly. Like a snowball rolling downhill, that opinion can easily grow so large that talking alone cannot stop it.

That's why I'd want my contact to have a tangible tool to help them in that situation.

For Gyrus, the tool those contacts were given was a six pages long. On the first page were the five key benefits of their solution, in a way where each was a mini-billboard. If you even glanced at the paper, these business-oriented advantages popped out.[*]

Behind it, each of those key benefits had its own page. This fleshed out those benefits, but in a way that was easy to use in a meeting setting.

Deliberately, it wasn't fancy – it was printed on ordinary white paper – but it sure was effective.

[*] You may have to create this yourself – your engineering and marketing departments may not be able to resist packing in too much.

Helping Your Contact Champion Your Sale

Giving your contact a mini-presentation on paper – like I did for Gyrus – will give them added confidence in that decision committee meeting.*

In such a setting, the person with hardcopy in front of them tends to have more credibility than one who is merely talking from memory. The next step is to create desire so your contact will want to bring it to the meeting.

We coached Gyrus' salespeople to serve it up this way:

Words That Work:
 "Here's something I've created that you may find very useful once the meeting is underway. The first page says it all; the rest are just supporting details.

"It's simple, but it captures the five key points we've talked about that we have found matter to executives. In the committee meeting, you may find it very helpful to have if the situation calls for it."

When possible, the salesperson even provided their contact with multiple copies so they would have them on hand to pass out at the meeting if they decided they wanted to.

All the Gyrus salespeople immediately began using this approach and tool. It was originally devised to save one particularly important sale, which it did. Within three months, this approach had more than doubled their success rate when decision committees were involved.

* See previous section.

Chapter 4

The Technology Salesperson's Toolkit

No one has to tell you how even a phrase or question at the right moment can change everything. You already know many approaches and techniques; this section will add even more to your toolkit.

These are all tested and proven – they come from my work with thousands of technology sales professionals. You will learn ways to stay important, how to make references pay off, specifics for selling emerging technologies and how to reach even 'unreachable' executives.

Throughout, you will find <u>Words That Work</u> that you can adapt in your sales situations.

Knowing more techniques means having more options in challenging sales situations. I'm sure you will use these time and again – but the beauty of knowing more is that the first time one delivers a single incremental sale, you already have a great ROI.

Educating for Free?

If you're trying to sell an exciting emerging technology, there will be plenty of technical people at target accounts who would like to learn all about it.

How many? Enough to go broke. Here's a story of how to get out of the "free-education-thanks-but-no-purchase" business.

IBM's Lotus Notes has been very successful for the company and thousands of channel partners, but there was a time when it was on the verge of sinking. In the first year, that channel only had 200 channel partners across North America, consisting of system integrators, VARs and consultants. Those salespeople found plenty of prospects eager to learn more, but those many meetings were not turning into sales. Less than a year in, many in the channel were on the verge of dropping out.

I learned about this when I was asked to be the keynote at Lotus' first partner conference. My speech went over very well and within a week I received a call from Al Stoddard, the executive in charge of their channel partner program, asking me to immediately create and lead tactical workshops for partners across North America.

Timing was important. Within three months, I had developed the workshop and partners were already being trained. The workshops were intensive, practical and comprehensive; much was covered and practiced in each.

But one pivotal tactic brought immediate results – it literally changed the way partners sold and dramatically improved sales.

- -

Create Desire – Not Students, Not Admirers

I first helped the partner salespeople see the problem, so they could then turn around those meetings. I explained,

"When prospects ask – as they always do – 'What is Notes?', the best response is not to dive in to explain the technology. As you know firsthand, that doesn't lead to orders – it leads to more technical meetings. That's not helping you, and it's not helping that company.

"So since you're not getting paid to educate them, change your goal* for that meeting. You need to <u>create desire</u> and get them motivated to bring business areas to the next meeting."

"So when they ask, What is Notes, answer this way…"

They were then taught the better approaches and <u>Words That Work</u>. Next came no-pressure small group role play where they could practice their own style before trying it with customers.

The impact was huge.[**] The salespeople were all bright and accomplished, but they never realized they had the option – no, the obligation – to guide the customer instead of only educating.

Every great solution – including yours – can be explained in several ways. Some, however, will be much better than others at creating desire, expanding the audience, and shortening the sale cycle.

---

* See 'Goals vs. Non-Goals' in Chapter 3; this is a perfect example.

** Worldwide SVP of Sales Deb Besemer credited this work as being instrumental in the company's success.

What If the Customer Insists?

The temptation to explain any new and exciting technology like Lotus Notes is hard to resist.

The goal, however, is to sell it.

Was I suggesting the salesperson should *refuse* to explain about how Notes accomplished these amazing things? Not at all. But they now knew a far better way than *leading* with tech talk. It immediately changed their sales cycle; second meetings now included business people with problems to solve (or dreams to make real) and money to do it.

What if that first contact tried to insist on a technical educational session? They'd hear that channel salesperson say, with a smile:

Words That Work:
"I could delve into the technology for hours – but unless there's a real business need here for what this technology can deliver for you, I'd hate to waste your time on that."

This approach worked – in every country around the world.[*]

Did business partners profit from this better way of selling this emerging technology? Lotus VP Don Bulens put it this way, *"Many of our channel partners became millionaires because of Ken Wax."*

---

[*] The workshop was so successful that I eventually taught it in over 20 cities on five continents, including to both channel salespeople and IBM's direct sales Software Account Managers.

Selling Emerging Technologies

Selling technology is always challenging. Selling emerging technology is even harder – it should be virtually impossible.

Yet I've met and counseled hundreds of highly successful salespeople who do it year after year. Here are five points I share with them.

1. Don't Fool Yourself

At your company, everyone has already grown comfy with this new technology. You folks are living slightly in the future. Over at your prospect's organization, that's not the case. While someone may be intrigued, they start with a very different mindset. Every brand new technology has to sell to old-version humans.

2. Establish the Dream (or Problem) First

Never forget that your prospect's company has survived and thrived up until now without your new technology. If you want to become a priority, you really have to get them envisioning how life will be better (and subtly, the heroes made) thanks to your new solution.

This step shouldn't be rushed. Clearly paint the picture of the effect on day-to-day business, marketplace impact – whatever your new technology will dramatically improve.

3. Translate the Status Quo Into Ongoing Costs or Risks

Drive that impact home by having them appreciate how the costs of doing things the old way will keep piling up, or how not seizing this opportunity leaves them vulnerable if and when their competitors do.

Words That Work:

"What we hear from other customers is that they did the math and saw no reason to keep wasting that money month after month. [*] *"*

"If you agree that this is something everyone will have sooner or later, I'd love to have your company benefiting from it sooner rather than later – particularly in your competitive field."

Now we're getting beyond techno-lust to an impact that might make your contact a hero. Plus you've taught them points they can use to champion this internally.

4. Avoid Touching the Third Rail

Resist focusing on how your solution can allow them to reduce staff. It's an uncomfortable topic; no one wants to be the person who got Harry and Sue fired because of the new automated solution. Plus there's that karma thing – might the next efficiency axe fall on me?

Instead, talk about the workplace improvements and marketplace advantages, and how your solution will free up people to do things that aren't getting done, or could bring in more revenue.

Words That Work:

"Imagine the impact when you can free your people up for more creative and valuable work. Imagine how that will allow you to..."

5. Repeat as Necessary

Once isn't enough. If your solution is new and unfamiliar, you should mention those big ideas and benefits at every interaction.

---

* You might want to do the math for them. Here's a simple example: If your solution will save or earn them, say, $100 a week, multiply that by 52; now we're talking thousands of dollars every year into the future. Simple but effective.

Serving Up Services

Customers see services differently than they view hardware or software. While all three come under the same 'technology umbrella', you need to focus on different things when selling services.

Why is this? From the customer's point of view:

Services are *Really* Intangible: More so than software or hardware. The customer can't hold services, can't peek under the hood, and can't easily compare them with other models.

Services are Far Less Predictable: Unlike hardware or software, services don't come off an assembly line. There are no manuals to read, no objective reviews to bring confidence.

Quality Assurance is Impossible: While manufactured products go through extensive quality assurance, there's no such equivalent with services.

Services are Inconsistent: Every piece of hardware or software that comes off the production line is identical. But services depend on which individual is working on your project today and tomorrow.

Services are all about people. When a customer is buying services, they're really buying your company.

That means the quality of services hinges on what individuals know and can do, and how effectively and quickly they can do it.

This, in turn, means your services sale hinges on how well you convey and differentiate that knowledge and competence.

It also explains why customers remain cautious even despite the often-heard claim, *"What makes us unique? Oh, we've got the best people!"*[*]

When I work with sales teams, here are some of the things we cover and practice:

Sell Your People
And don't be shy about it. Don't just say that you've got highly trained people. Such empty claims can be made by your competitors.

Instead, make your technical experts real – have the customer feel like he or she already knows them. Tell a brief story about how one of them made an impact at a customer. Name names, and convey pride in how their training and experience made a hero at that account.

Detail Where Their Expertise Comes From
Talk about where they've been and what they've seen. Talk up the complex projects they've handled masterfully. If yours is a smaller company, and some of your people worked previously at well-known large system integrators, you might want to mention it. Talk about the ongoing training they get and any conferences they attend.

Have a Kicker
Don't just say they did a good job at an account – point out something they noticed and improved that went beyond the call of duty.

Here an example of how **Flexible Business Systems** does that when selling to small businesses. The salesperson might explain the case

---

[*] Customers rightfully ask themselves: If every services company claims they have "the best people", then where do all the mediocre ones work?

----

where their technical people solved an intermittent router problem that had previously been 'unsolvable' by other companies.

Then they add this kicker: While on the project, their folks went beyond the call of duty and checked the data plan that customer had with the phone company. They determined it was far more than that company needed. Because of this, that customer changed their plan with the phone company and immediately began saving $600 every month – over $7,000 every year.

If you were a small business owner, isn't that the kind of care and expert initiative you'd want?

Use the Halo Effect

It can be valuable to briefly mention some very complex projects your people have done at big companies, even to customers whose needs are far more humble. It brings great confidence to know such mastery will be brought to work on their projects.

Make your services personal – highlight the individuals, make the customer feel for their accomplishments and professionalism. This is what the customer needs to differentiate your company and move ahead with confidence.

References, Premature

"Well can you give me a few references I can talk to?"

It's such an easy question to ask – even on a first meeting, even if they're not really serious. Who knows, they may even think it's the polite or expected thing to do.

Careful here. At this early point, how relevant are the comments of a total stranger? Not very. Besides, this prospect isn't far enough along in the process to even know what to ask that reference.

References at the wrong time, even great ones, can actually slow down a sale. Don't allow them to come into play too early. Even when the time is right, you shouldn't just hand over their contact information; doing so creates three problems:

1. Tired References
References are a limited resource. Even if I am your biggest fan, at a certain point I've had enough of talking to strangers for you. If I feel I'm wasting my time doing this, I cease being that reference for you.

2. Lost Opportunities
Will they actually connect up and talk? Often, they won't. Your prospect calls me and leaves a message. I call back and leave another message. Or I forget. Either way your sale is not moving ahead.

3. Not Impressed
Customers rarely like to talk about their past inefficiencies, or may be using your technology to gain a competitive advantage. As such, comments may be vague. Your prospect is unimpressed. You don't know what happened; all you know is that the prospect is not returning your calls.

References, Done Right

When a prospect asks for references too early in the sales cycle, you owe it to them and your sale to guide them:

<u>Words That Work:</u>
"We certainly have many happy customers who can give you insight into their experiences. But I'd like to suggest we wait until we are further along in the process before doing that.

"One reason is that I'd like to connect you up with not just any references, but ones who will be of value to you. Only when we get closer to the details of this project can that be done. To just give you the names and number of strangers now wouldn't be nearly as useful.

"Another reason is that we are very respectful of our references' time. If we do business and you become one of those references, I'm sure you will appreciate that."

"Lastly, I want to do this right.

"The people we use as references are rarely at their desks with free time. Instead of handing you a phone number and hoping you can connect, I will personally speak with them to arrange a convenient time and ensure the reference knows what areas might be of most interest and value to you. That way, I make sure neither of you waste time playing phone tag."

This approach serves everyone. It's best for you, your references, and for that prospect. Anyone who balks after hearing those reasons wasn't serious in the first place.

Laws of Objections*

1. Every Objection is 100% Absolutely Valid

(To the person who raises it)

2. An Objection Can Only Be Removed by the Person Who Raises It

(That means you can't use 'force of facts' to prove them wrong.

You may be able to address it, or answer it – but the key to success is to bring them an insight that will open their mind. Only when they decide to reevaluate that cherished objection can they happily abandon it and let the sale move ahead.)

* These are good to review before any important meeting.

Let Me Tell You a Story

When you were a child, did your parents read you the story of Goldilocks and the Three Bears? Or did they read you the spec sheet?

- 3 Bowls

- 3 Bears

- 3 Chairs

- 1 Blonde

Of course they didn't, even though the spec sheet would have been much quicker than telling the story.

We humans are built for stories. For thousands of years, that's pretty much all we had. They appeal to our imagination and have us envisioning ourselves in that situation.

When I'm giving a speech I know that I will get everyone's attention with, *"Let me tell you a story about that..."*

Technically oriented folks often think stories in selling are pointless. Why waste time with them when all that matters is the specs, the data behind such fluff? Because you're selling to humans. They need stories and if you want them to expand your sale, so do you.

I've taught thousands of technical salespeople how to tell compelling stories[*] about their product, their company and their benefits – and I've seen the impact.

---

[*] Case studies aren't stories; we'll cover that in the next section.

Here's why stories make such an impact:

They're Easy to Tell, Easy to Remember

That's crucial in selling, since so much hinges on whether your sale will grow to include others. If your initial contact hears and remembers a relevant story, they help advance your sale every time they retell it.

All Stories, However, Are Not Equal

The only ones that get retold are the interesting ones. Don't waste time on ones that are predicable, as in, "Here's a company that bought from us, and we say they like it." Find stories where there was some unexpected additional benefit at the end.

For Impact, Make It Personal

Focus on the people, not the technology. Make them feel for the person who brought in your solution and the appreciation they received for that smart move. That's what gets them envisioning good things happening to them if they move this sale along.

You Must Name Names (But You've Got Some Flexibility)

Unattributed stories have little credibility. But what do you do if there is a terrific success story you'd love to use but that customer forbids you using their name?

First tell two stories about named companies. Doing this gives you the credibility to introduce the unnamed one this way:

Words That Work:
"My last story is from a company who doesn't want their name mentioned, and we, of course, respect that. But I think you will find their experience particularly relevant to your goals, so let me tell it without identifying them."

You actually get an added benefit – they now know that if they become customers you won't name them unless allowed.

How to Get Started

You probably have at least one or two good examples from accounts of yours. Next, ask a few of the top salespeople which examples they use. You might also check the case studies your company has; track down who had that account and ask them to tell you about it in their own words.

Brevity is the Key

Time yourself while you say it out loud. If you can't tell it in under two minutes, make it shorter. A story's job is to spark a conversation, not to give a dissertation.

It's Crucial That You Practice Out Loud

Every Broadway show has rehearsals. There must be a reason why they don't save time and money by letting the actors read silently and then show up on opening night. Storytelling is all about comfort; there is no substitute for practicing out loud. Easiest place to do it: your car.

Why Case Studies Don't Cut It

Case studies aren't stories.

Most are anything but. They're usually dry, approved-by-legal dissertations with quotes no human would ever say. They may have their place, but rare is the one that will motivate people to buy.

As I've suggested, using a case study as the *basis* for a story can make sense. You already have names and information; now you need to make it intriguing and then satisfying.

Start by Digging Around – Find the person who had that account or who wrote up the original story.

Focus On the People – Learn who was 'in the boat' for this to happen, and what happened afterwards.[*]

Use the Case Information, But Creatively – For example, you may have tell the story backwards.

Words That Work:
"I'm going to tell you a short story where the ending has a savings of almost a million dollars, and someone gets promoted."

Now you have their attention!

---

[*] If the person who championed your sale earned a promotion, mention it every time.

Toughest Questions, Never Fearing

If you sell technology, you're going to get surprised. It's not a matter of if; it's just a question of when.

No matter how well trained or brilliant you may be, there will be times when you hear a question that has you fumbling. So don't beat yourself up too much when it happens.

But, as the saying goes, you don't learn much the *second* time you get kicked by a mule.

When a question surprises you, decide at that very moment that this will be the last time that particular question will ever be a problem for you.

After that interaction, ask whoever in your company might know the best answer. Don't be shy about it; I would ask other salespeople or my boss, *"I was caught off guard when a prospect asked ... I want to be masterful next time anyone poses that. What do you think is the best way to handle that?"*

Learn everything you can, craft a terrific approach to take the next time that question comes up. Practice and master your answer.

Then the next time that question comes up, you're set. The hardest thing you'll have to do is stifle a knowing smile because you're so ready to knock this out of the ballpark.

Tough Questions, Big Meeting

Tough questions can also be compounded by timing.

You may be in a big meeting with several key decision makers and a difficult question comes out of left field. What should you do when caught off guard in an important meeting? It all depends on the specifics. Here are some guidelines:

Don't Try Bluffing
Experienced business people can sense that as easily as you can tell when a child is lying. No point in losing all your credibility.

Treat It Calmly
Simply pick up your pen and say,

Words That Work:
"I'm not certain and I don't want to risk giving you wrong information, so let me make note of that and get back to you."

Avoid saying things like, *"That's a good question."*, or *"Hmm, I've never heard that before."* – they gain you nothing.

Don't Stop Everything
Think twice before offering to call someone right now who might have the answer. Such delays are awkward and people tend to leave while this happens.

"Let's Assume We Can Solve It"
Don't let it derail the meeting. If you can't answer it now, try to proceed as if the answer, when you ascertain it, will be the right one.

Words That Work.
"How about we assume the answer will be precisely what you want. If that's the case, what needs to happen to move this ahead?"

103

Ken Wax vs. Brad Pitt

Some people think all problems can be solved with a comparison chart. You know the type – where your wonderful product has check marks for everything, but competitors have columns that are half-empty. If we only had one, the yearning goes, it would make it clear to customers how superior we are.

Don't count on it.

Customers have learned that the company who makes the categories always wins the comparison. That's why a checklist should never be the backbone of your sales pitch; it's just not strong enough.

But what if your checklist advantages are truly remarkable? Doesn't that make a checklist strong enough to influence others?
No, just the opposite – because of that lopsided outcome it is even less likely to be shared with others.[*]

"But They're Objective Facts!"
That's the defense. But who says they're objective? Would the losing competitors on that checklist agree it was a fair and representative comparison? Of course not.

Years ago I developed the following checklist for a talk I was giving in Palo Alto for the Silicon Valley Entrepreneurs Club. Imagine it being created on an easel as you watch.

"Let's see why checklist comparisons rarely have the credibility with prospects that they have back at the office."

[*] "Hey boss, look, their comparison says really good things about them!"

I then quickly draw the blank table.

	Ken Wax	Brad Pitt

"Let's compare Ken Wax with Brad Pitt, with all data being accurate, of course. Let's see which of the two comes out on top."

Then, I announce our data points and fill in the chart. The excitement builds, bringing us to my conclusion:

	Ken Wax	Brad Pitt
Size 11 Shoe	YES!	No
Amateur Magician	YES!	No
Owns Most Computers	YES!	No

"So, based on this objective analysis, it is clear who is the more desirable male." (I am quick to add, *"Except that over 3 billion women might disagree."*)

Depending on your sale, checklists probably have a place for spotlighting features and functionality. They can help provide the tech-spec justification your contacts may need internally. Use it as the tool it is, but don't expect too much from your checklist.

Selling When Attacked

There will be times when you find yourself in a meeting where someone is trying their hardest to undermine you and your solution.

Maybe they're biased towards another vendor or are showing off for someone else in the meeting. It could be a game to them or a negotiating ploy.

Whatever the reason – and you will probably never know – you are in an awkward spot. If you directly rebut them, they may see it as a personal attack. Proving them wrong may win the moment but lose the sale.

You're stuck. If you don't try something new right now, this will be your last meeting with them. Here's a tack to take:

Words That Work:
"I'm hearing a lot of concerns. On one hand, that's good; it means you're looking for the right solution for your company. On the other, I'm not sure it's good for any relationship we might have for us to be having such a challenging discussion."

Pause for a second, to collect your thoughts.

"If it's okay with you, I'd like to briefly raise a point, then ask you all a question."

Pause again; you're awaiting permission. That's important. It's their conversation too, and you're asking if it's okay to come at it in a different way. You will quickly get a nod or comment that it's okay; I've never been in a situation where it wasn't allowed.

Words That Work:
"The point is this. While I'm not saying it automatically means we're right for you, as you probably know we have been chosen by companies like ..., ... and ...."

Quickly rattle off three companies they will recognize. It might be companies the same size, in the same industry, or in their area. Then:

"Now most people would agree these aren't all foolish companies. They've got sharp people who looked long and hard and then decided to do business with us. It's been a good experience; I can connect you up with the key people over there if you'd like.

"In the time we have left in this meeting, is there any way we can focus on the good things our solution is doing for them and other companies, and would be able to do for you?"

Once you pose that, there are only a limited number of outcomes.

1. They will remain contentious.

This is hard to do, since you've offered an olive branch to defuse the acrimony. You've also pointed out how other companies somehow didn't see all these shortcomings. If they stay in fighting mode, it's likely there's a hidden agenda here; you never really had a chance.

2. Someone in the meeting will agree to change the tone.

Usually it's the highest ranking person in the meeting. You've made it easy for the meeting to return to civility and move ahead.

You'll hear a comment along the lines of, *"Well, we will need to explore those areas at some point, but for now, why not tell us more about what you're doing for (one of the companies you'd mentioned)."*

It's a great feeling. You've just saved the meeting, and maybe the sale.

Obstacles, Unmentioned

Sometimes the biggest obstacle to a sale never gets voiced in a meeting. How can you deal with it if you don't even know about it?

There is a way.

One of my clients, **USConnect** was very successful in selling services. While not nearly the size of the largest system integrators, they had hundreds of employees in offices all over North America, often winning against the giants in that field.

The problem, CEO Ed Groark explained it to me, was when no one mentioned those giants.

Sometimes USConnect learned the reason they'd lost a project was because, after the meeting, someone voiced a concern that they couldn't deliver specialists like the big guys could.

If they had asked the salesperson, they would have learned that, yes, USConnect did have such experts, many who came from those big integrators. Plus they would have learned that their company would have received the attention of far more senior talent than the big integrators typically assign to mid-size accounts.

But no one asked. You can't speak to issues that only get voiced after the meeting is over.

Here's what I taught the USConnect sales team to say towards the end of any meeting when they sensed they were competing with the big integrators:

Words That Work:
"I hope I've covered all the areas you were expecting and answered every one of your questions. What I'd like to ask right now is, are

there any areas, any areas at all, that you have questions or concerns about?

"Because if you do, it's important to get them on the table so we can discuss them. I'm sure none of us wants to have a situation where after the meeting you say, 'Gee, I had a question but didn't bring it up'.

"So are there any questions or areas we should cover?"

Then wait until someone says, *"No, we're good."* It will usually be the highest ranking person in the meeting.

Or you may hear, *"Well..."* and then they'll voice those previously unmentioned doubts. You've made it easy for them to bring them up and now you get to speak to those issues.

Here's an additional plus of this approach: Suppose there is someone who, for whatever the reason, wanted to undermine your sale. He remains quiet when you ask to hear all concerns, waiting until after you're gone to wonder aloud if your company is, say, big enough to handle the job properly.

Because you were so clear about asking about concerns, odds are good he will be met with a terse, *"Well then why didn't you mention that at the meeting instead of keeping quiet?"* Gone is the manipulative impact he would have had otherwise.

Guys on Horses

At the circus, you know when something big and important is about to happen. The ringmaster tells you.

He steps into the spotlight and in a booming, clearly excited voice announces,

"Next, in the center ring, from the far flung reaches of outer Mongolia, the amazing, death defying Vernado Brothers on their golden palominos!"

Everyone leans forward as they come out galloping in a circle, all eyes are riveted so as not to miss a second of what undoubtedly will be sheer excitement. The ringmaster promised that in his introduction and you are ready to receive.

But what if, instead, the ringmaster's introduction consisted of him meekly uttering,

"Now, guys on horses."?

Same brothers, same horses. But introduced that way, who cares?

In sales interactions, you are the ringmaster. Whether it's on the phone, web meeting, or in person, your prospects are trying to figure out the most important points. Tell them.

Let's use a simplified example. Suppose your solution has capabilities that allow training modules to be quickly created in-house, as opposed to contracting with outside specialists. You could just say that. But that's like saying, *"Now, guys on horses."*

Instead, why not set it up in a way that tells them this is important to them and companies like theirs?

Words That Work:

"What I'm about to tell you is an advance that has changed time-to-market at several customers of ours – while reducing costs by hundreds of thousands of dollars.

"It's probably the single most leveraged thing a company your size could do to advance or even transform your response time in creating training materials."

Think that prospect is paying attention? You bet they are. This might make them a hero. Now that your introduction has them on the edge of their seat, your big benefit will get the attention it deserves.

Competitors, Criticizing Of

Careful here. Your credibility is at stake.

It's predictable that prospects will ask, *"How do you stack up against...?"*

I know I'd ask. Who better than you to point out the other guy's flaws? Even if I have no intention of buying from you, such information would be useful when time comes to negotiate with them.

Tempting as it may be to bash them, don't. Here's why:

1. This Prospect Already Has Opinions
What happens when your heartfelt critique is at odds with their already-formed opinion? You lose. You are either deemed ignorant or deceitful.

2. Nobody Likes a Basher
It's just poor form to speak ill of others. That's the case even if your slams are accurate and public knowledge. We rarely like people who berate others, probably because it raises the question of whether they might just as easily badmouth us if asked.

This doesn't mean you can't raise valid questions about the other guys. Very often, you should. By telling that prospect of areas worth exploring, it can help them make the best decision. But always do it gently – and always with the following caveat:

Words That Work:
"I won't claim to be an expert on their products or claims; all I can tell you is what I've heard from people at my accounts. I do know that customers who have gone with us mention that they were concerned about..."

Then point out whatever needs to be brought up. But you've clearly established that you're not here to slam. And you have also identified your critiques as significant enough that people at other companies chose your solution.

Of course, you'd better be sure these are accurate criticisms. Wrap up with:

Words That Work:
"As I said, I'm not pretending to be an expert on their strengths or weaknesses. I'll leave it to you to do your own 'due diligence', but I do know those items have come up from companies who have chosen us and you might want to investigate them."

Yes, you've raised some doubts about that competitor – but in a properly professional way where your only goal was to help your contact.

Show Them Their Future

Learn how to become a time machine and you will transform your sales impact. Take your prospects slightly into the future, to feel what life will be like once they begin benefiting from your solution.

You will shorten your sales cycle by having them envision the results once your solution is up and running. Once they can 'see' that future, returning to the present is a step backwards.

Set it up this way:

Words That Work:
"What I'd like to do for a moment is bring you something from my other customers who have already implemented this – insight into what your day-to-day experience will be once this is up and running.

"Right now, as I understand it, you... (state current limitations or ongoing costs of status quo that they've told you.) As we've seen at other customers of ours, soon you will no longer have that. Instead,...(now paint picture of life with your solution)."

Continue on as appropriate. The whole thing should take only a minute or two. But you will have engaged that most potent of tools – their imagination.

"We're in No Rush"

"Well, we're in no rush about this. Maybe later this year, or next."

Procrastinating is a very popular option.[*] It often happens because people who live all their days deep within a corporation have forgotten that there's a world out there beyond their company.

Let's help remind them. With an understanding smile and in no way challenging, give them food for thought:

Words That Work:
"Well, that's certainly your prerogative, every company has to decide what should be a priority and when to seize opportunities.

"But you might want to ask yourself, 'What's going on right now at my key competitors?' Because in all likelihood, there are people there with the exact same jobs you have, facing the same choices as you.

"Unless you're certain that your competitors are also in no rush to add this capability, you may want to consider the impact if they move ahead while you don't."

This can change everything. Now let's make it real with an example.

"Let me give you an example outside your industry.[**] It was only a few years ago when distributors' websites listed products, but didn't show, in real time, what was in stock and available to ship."

---

[*] Especially when it comes to tech purchases, which almost always get better and cheaper if one waits.

[**] If you use an example in their field right now, chances are they will either get distracted thinking about it, or might try to poke holes in your example.

"As that technical ability became possible, some distributors said they were in no rush. But others didn't delay.

"What happened? Just as you'd expect. When customers of the 'We're in no rush' company placed orders, they would frequently find out the next day that, sorry, part of their order was out of stock.

"So when they heard that some other distributors now were showing real-time availability, they tried it and liked it – and switched.

"Soon the 'no rush' distributors were losing customers and were in a big rush. Plus they now had to spend a small fortune to try and win back customers who had switched away.

"I mention this because I'd like to see you folks benefiting from...(solution), and not finding yourselves vulnerable when senior executives learn that other competitors are adding this capability.

You've certainly given them something to think about! Now it's time to make it easy for them to move ahead:

Words That Work:.
"Isn't there some way we can get some sort of trial or pilot program started, so you can at least point to it if anyone in senior management asks why your competitors can now do things that your company can't?"

Done right, this should get them revisiting their strategy of waiting. You are certainly doing them a favor by pointing out their vulnerability if they continue with their postponement plans.

Equally important, you've just taught them how to sell others inside their company. It's now much easier for them to campaign for funding; they can tell the distributor-impact story and look visionary as they do.

"Your Price is Too High"

It always is. Price is the easiest challenge to pose. No need for insights or substantiation; all you need to do is utter those five magic words and see what happens.

An inexperienced salesperson may take the bait. *"Hmm, let me see – if we bring it in for, say, ___, would we have a deal?"*

They think they're being nice and helpful. But it's called negotiating against oneself . Even lowering your price to a number they suggest without a solid justification can cause problems. Watch.

Suppose you've got a solution priced at, say, $100,000. Your contact balks at that price, asking you reduce it to $85,000. Which you do. Which of these thoughts are likely to be going through the mind of that prospect?

> a) *"Wow, I got $15,000 shaved off. I feel great!"*

> b) *"I was a pushover; I should have asked for $25,000 off."*

No one is happy. Not only that, but you've trained them to hold out for a lower price every time they do business with you in the future.

What can you do when price is cited as the stumbling block?

1. Don't Retreat, Justify
If your pricing is fair, you shouldn't be ashamed of it.

Remind them of the experience you folks have, the high value received for money spent, and specifics of what they're getting for their investment.

----

2. Cite How Other Customers Find It Worth the Money

Mention six or eight other accounts who have bought and who find it to be well worth the investment. Don't be shy about this. It reminds the prospect of your experience and puts them on the defensive – now they need to justify why they think your price is not reasonable.

3. Make the Analogy to Their Business

Words That Work:

"Just like your company, we provide a quality product, price it accordingly and have many happy customers. You provide solid value for the prices you charge your customers – that's why you've been successful – and so do we."*

4. Let Them Know That to Pay Less Means to Get Less

Yes, you can lower the price, but it won't be the identical solution. Analogy: to pay less for a car, you give up certain luxuries. Many times you'll hear them acknowledging that they really do need all that was in the full proposal. The sale will go through as proposed.

5. Tell Them What They Will Have to Add

While you will have to check back at the office**, you might be able to lower the price if they do some aspects, or give you flexibility in scheduling the project to fit your needs.

No salesperson ever wants to lower price, but sometimes there's no choice. Done properly, your contact is a hero, you are appreciated, and they haven't been trained to expect it every time. Everybody wins.

---

* See 'We Need You to Lower Your Price', later in the chapter.

** This makes it much more credible, while giving you flexibility at the same time.

"We Found Someone Cheaper"

What do you do if prospects tell you about a competitor that has an *identical* product, yet is lower in price?

PCR had that problem. Theirs is a low-tech part of the technology business: renting PCs. This happens to be a surprisingly big business, catering to the shifting seasonal or growth needs of corporations and how accounting rules treat those computers.

At a speech I was giving for their 120 North American franchise owners, they posed a provocative question:

"What do you think we should be doing when local companies undercut our prices?"

The murmur that followed told me this was an important problem for them.

I asked what they currently did when that happens.
"We match their price."

We discussed it for a while, then I shook up the room. Keep in mind, this was costing them every day, not to mention making them feel helpless. The fact that these cut-rate competitors quickly went out of business was no consolation; a new one would arise.

I then asked the group what they thought would happen if they instead said to that customer:

Words That Work:
"Look, in this business, there are no secrets. We all pay the same for PCs. The trucks we need to deliver them cost the same to run. Every company has to pay for support people who get those PCs installed and then take care of you by fixing any problems that may arise.

"There's only one way a company can offer you a substantially lower price – something has to give. Corners must be cut – there's simply no other way.

"It might be the staffing of the support team. Or by having a longer response time to replace a problem machine because they have fewer trucks, drivers, or backup machines. In most cases, you don't find out about the corners they've cut until you have a problem and it impacts your business.

"You have to ask yourself, 'What am I using these PCs for?' 'How much am I paying in salaries to the people who are using them?' 'What's the impact on our business if they're sitting there idle because of the 'discount resource' we chose? '

" I think you will find that compared to the important work you will be using these machines for, the weekly difference is trivial.

"That's why we have so many companies counting on us. Companies like,..., ..., and... They care about the weekly rental cost, sure. But they're deciding by also considering the value of knowing your team will have the functioning equipment you're counting on them having."

There was silence for a second, then applause burst out.

For weeks and even months afterwards, I received notes from those franchise owners.

Whether you're selling technology or ice cream, there will always be lower price competitors. Your job is to have your prospects see that there's a very good reason they value themselves that way.

Competing Against "Free!"

Competing against a cheaper competitor is easy – but what about one that's free?

That was the problem that **ATG** faced when technology giant SAP began offering a competing portal product at no cost.

I had worked with ATG before, teaching their sales teams in the North America, Europe and Asia.[*] This portal product was a strategic one for them. It was priced attractively; no serious prospect would balk at the cost. But when a huge company like SAP dangles one for free, that changes everything.

The real problem here for the customer isn't about the money – it's about *explaining*. What do you say if a senior manager asks why you want to spend money on something that appears similar to one that an industry giant will provide at no charge?

If you can't confidently answer that question, you are going to choose the free one.

It's tempting for the salesperson to dive in listing reasons why that free one isn't as good. That may be the case, but it doesn't address the problem their prospect is facing. If he or she is challenged internally, listing technical details will likely bring, *"Are you saying SAP's won't do most of the things we need?"* Not a good spot to be in.

[*] See 'Follow the Money', Chapter 2

What's the Real Cost of Free?

Let's role play. I'm the salesperson, and you've just told me, *"I do like your portal technology, but SAP will give us theirs for free."*

You see me pause to take that in; it's clear that I'm thinking about it. Then I look across the table and earnestly ask you:

Words That Work:

"Hmm. Why do you think they're doing that? I mean, why would a company like them choose to value their portal that way?"

Then I don't say another word. What is going through your head?

As the customer, you can't help thinking – and in this case, saying aloud – reasons like:

- *"It could be because their portal has flaws and that no one was willing to pay for it."*
- *"Either that or they're going to make the money up, and more, with services."*
- *"Or choosing it might somehow lock us into buying additional things from them."*
- *"Or..."*

The key here is that these are the customer's insights – not arguments given by a salesperson. That's important; it brings great confidence. Should anyone inside their organization ask, *"Why not get the free one?"*, all they have to do is think out loud again.

This thinking on the part of your contact changes everything. Now, anyone who suggests choosing the freebie is taking a personal risk – it's up to them to make a very compelling case for accepting a free product and whatever strings may later be found to be attached to it.

"We Need You to Lower Your Price"

"We like you, but I have to tell you. We have another resource whose price is lower. You're not the cheapest, and price is important to us."

It's awkward whenever a prospect you've been working with tries to get you to lower your price.* If this squeeze comes from a manager in a meeting where you are outnumbered, it is even more problematic.

What do you do?

If you simply refuse to drop your price, that manager now looks weak. They could say okay, but more likely they will tell you the whole purchase is now in jeopardy. Now you're stuck.

Inexperienced salespeople may try explaining that they don't have the power to change pricing. The hope is that will end the discussion and result in the sale. More likely, they'll say to get your boss involved – and the sale is on hold until you do.

Let's keep matters in perspective. There must be a reason why you've reached this advanced point: They truly want what you're selling. That's why they've invested time and energy. If they were so enamored with a lower-priced competitor, they would have already bought from them and this meeting wouldn't be taking place.

With that in mind, here's an approach you may find very useful. I know for a fact it has saved millions of dollars over the years I have been teaching it.

---

* See 'Your Price is Too High' for five tactics.

With a smile in your voice, in a friendly, non-confrontational way, say,

Words That Work:
"Oh, I can understand you wanting a lower price. I wish we could do the project for you for free.*

"But of course, we can't – just as your company can't provide your products for free or below your costs. At least not if you want to stay in business.

"My guess is that when your company's customers ask for even lower prices, your salespeople explain the value of doing business with you – even though your products are not the cheapest in the market.

"It's the same with us. As I've hopefully conveyed in working with (names of all the people you've met with), we bring you experience and expertise – and confidence in success. That's a big part of our value, just as it is probably a big reason why your company's customers choose to do business with you.

"The pricing we've worked out is fair; it's the same structure we've used with companies such as …, … and … While, as I said, I wish we could do it for free or below our costs, I don't think that's how your company does business, plus it wouldn't really be fair to all the other companies who have seen fairness and value in our pricing and the results we bring.

"I'd love to get this project moving ahead so you can begin benefiting from it sooner rather than later. As we've seen, it will save you … once it is up and running and I'd hate to have you waste another week or month before getting those savings and efficiencies.

---

* This is a remarkably useful phrase.

Words That Work:

"I know you will be as satisfied as our other customers, and as proud of the results and value you get. We know what it takes to do the job right and, that's how we arrive at our pricing, just as your company does."

What has just happened?   By presenting it this way, you avoid a confrontation. You've aligned your company with theirs. They well know their company isn't the cheapest in their market, yet customers happily buy from them. If that's fair for them and their pricing, it's hard to argue that it's not fair for you.

Your goal here is for that key person to smile and say, *"Well I guess that makes sense."* Which it does.

Lowering Price, If You Must

No one likes doing it, but there are times when you simply must lower the price in order to bring in the sale.

As we've seen earlier in this chapter, one rule regarding lowering your price is to always have them give up something in exchange. But if that's impossible, maybe you can have them 'give up' something that is free to them yet arguably valuable to you. Here's one way to do that:

Words That Work:
 "Well Bill, for reasons I've explained, we don't put 'cushion' into our pricing, which is why I can't lower it.

"But I may have a solution – I'll have to check – tell me what you think.

"I believe our Marketing people are still involved in a program that involves interviewing and getting quotes from customers. If you'd be willing to take a few minutes at certain stages during the project to share your impressions of working with us, we may * *be able to apply some of their marketing funds to this internally. In effect, that would lower your cost for this project."*

In most cases, they will happily agree. They're winning a lower price, yet all they're giving up in exchange is a bit of time.

By lowering your price this way, it is clearly a unique circumstance. They can't automatically ask for the same reduction on every future purchase. So while you've given them a lower price this time, you haven't trained them to expect it every time.

* You haven't offered this yet – only the possibility.

Lowering Price, Timing is Everything

When you agree to lower the price can be just as important as *how much*.

If you do it early on, you are setting the stage for requests for additional price cuts and concessions as the sale progresses.

If, for whatever the reason, you are raising the possibility of a discounted price, you want to first *wrap up everything else* about the deal. Otherwise, they're likely to ask for price adjustment on other things as discussions continue.

Words That Work:
"Let's assume, for the moment, that we can bring this in, in a way that fits in with your budget. What else has to happen to get you benefitting from this?"

This accomplishes an important goal – getting your conversation away from price. Now you're back to getting them envisioning owning your solution and benefitting from it.

Any price concessions should happen at the final stage. There's a good chance that once the customer has invested considerable time with you, and even introduced you and your solution to numerous others in their company, they may be less likely to negotiate on price – or will be less aggressive when they do.

Get Physical, Letters vs. Emails

I love email. Love it, love it, love it. Now that we've gotten that out of the way, I'd like you to consider the impact of a humble letter. You know, the type in an envelope that you have to rip open to read.

Here's why: I've trained plenty of salespeople who have earned enough money with this technique to buy a luxury car.

Countless times, I've heard back how the letter campaign tactic they learned in my workshop reached 'unreachable' executives. Their letters opened doors that emails never could.

Email is great for many things, but reaching busy strangers isn't one of them. Emails arrive in a parade of more important ones and are visually as plain as can be. Recipients are looking to delete them if possible so they can get back to work.

Now here's a question: *When was the last time you received a crisp letter at the office?* Ask that question of your Vice President or SVP. You will find that, even at their level, it's not very often.

No one gets letters anymore. That's why they can work wonders. Letters can reach people who would never read your emails. In fact, your envelope is welcome break from reading and deleting emails.

Your letter tells me things. It says you understand how to reach me. It proclaims I was worth the effort. These aren't trivial impressions. You now stand out from all the other email-sending salespeople.

Another plus: Your letter can travel in ways an email never would. If I'm a Director and the Vice President routes the letter you sent her to me, how likely is it that I will ignore it? Not very.

Letter Perfect

While it's true that a physical letter can reach and engage in ways no email ever can, that only happens when the letter is on-target and engaging. Here are some key points for putting the humble letter to work for you:

Short, Short, Short
Let me repeat that. Keep it short. If you want me to read it, it must be inviting. That means a single page, big margins, plenty of white space. Those few paragraphs then pop out and become irresistible.

Don't Sell, Intrigue
The goal is to spark my interest about a business area I care about, not to force feed me facts and claims. No one has time for a salesy, self-centered letter – and they sure won't be routing it to anyone.

Open With a Question
Why? That's how to open minds and draw people in.

It doesn't matter how dry the product may be – the right question can make it irresistible. **Clear Software**'s technology automatically turns text into flowcharts. I created a letter campaign that opened with, *"What would it be worth to your company if new employees made fewer mistakes?"* and it was sent out to senior executives at insurance companies, hospitals, manufacturers and other large enterprises. Within days, those executives had routed it to their directors and calls were coming in. Sales soared.

It's All About Your Offer
Make it easy for me to take the step you'd like. Appeal to my interests and make the offer specific. Don't merely ask for a meeting, don't just offer to give a presentation. It becomes more compelling if you instead offer, say, a 25 minute presentation on four changes others in my industry are making and why.

Leverage With Other Forms of Communication

Use the tools at your disposal. Have my phone number? Maybe leave me a very brief voicemail telling me you've just mailed me that letter. Sure, I'm going to quickly delete that message but I'm still more likely to notice your letter when it arrives.

Think: Coke

Everyone knows Coke.

Advertisers also know that a message must be repeated again and again. That's why Coke spends $71,232,876 on advertising *every single day*.[*] One letter may or may not reach and impress that target prospect. An ongoing campaign, however, will eventually achieve that goal.

---

[*] That was in 2006, the last year they disclosed this number. And, yes, you read it correctly —that's $71 million a day!

The $6 Solution

Hot prospects, as the saying goes, are like hot baths. Over time they should only be expected to grow cooler.

You know the feeling when a 'sure thing' in your pipeline forecast goes cold. Your sales manager sure knows the feeling of readjusting their projections when that happens.

The problem, of course, is that prospects proceed at their own pace. Often there is simply no way of rushing things. During this period, you want stay as close to them as possible, both to keep momentum and to prevent any competitors from making headway.

Those contacts, however, quickly grow weary of "just checking in!" phone messages and emails. Each time they delete you, you are slightly diminished.

Here's an inexpensive way to advance that sale or at least keep it from cooling off too much during that forced waiting period. A lot depends on your particular business of course, but the following can't be beat for simplicity, impact and cost-effectiveness.

1. Make up six envelopes addressed to that contact.

Including postage, these should cost you no more than $1 each

2. At regular intervals, send something.

You will find that by making up the envelopes in advance it take just seconds to slip something in and send it out.

What should you send?   Not salesy letters or literature. Instead, send a write-up of a success story, with a brief cover note along the lines of, *'Hi Lee, I thought you might find this interesting – their upper management is very impressed with the results.'*

Other possibilities: A reprint of a relevant news article or press release. Don't have any? Send another success story.

This simple program can be a secret weapon. Prospects can't help but grow impressed with your follow-through. Here's an added benefit of 'building the file': even if there's a reorg over there, that file folder of your mailings may help you quickly get noticed by the new person.

Too Much = Not Enough

Quick – memorize these three numbers: 4, 9, 20

Got it? Of course you do. Now try to remember these:

4, 6, 9, 11, 14, 16, 20, 23 and 26

Which set was easier?   Which one can be remembered more confidently?   The shorter one, of course.

What if I had instead asked you to remember three facts about my company or solution?   You could do it, with confidence. But if I had given you nine, probably not. If I had shown you 30, would you even try?

This is what every prospect has to deal with. When salespeople pile on too much, people quickly reach their limits. It all fuses together into a mess of information. They give up. No human could remember it all, and this human won't even be trying.

Which means they certainly won't be mentioning this to others.

5 Tactics When Emailing Contacts

Emails to your contacts are a useful tool, of course. But there's a problem: It's so easy and inexpensive and convenient – everyone does it. Again and again and again.

Your prospect gets far too many emails. Some are from higher-ups and peers, others from salespeople like you. Guess which ones are most easily ignored.

In a sense, every email you send to that person is telling them something about your value and whether you value their time.

That's why the smart salesperson uses email sparingly with existing contacts. You want each of your messages to be respected, and to get the attention and response it deserves.

When an email from you is deemed marginal and gets deleted, it means your contact saw that you'd written and decided you're not a priority right now. It's not the end of the world, at least not until they get in the habit of ignoring you.

Think of it this way: Every time your email is deleted or allowed to scroll away, your relationships dies a little.

So think twice before sending an email; look at it using your 'Customer Vision'. For example, does the subject line make clear what this is about and how urgent it is? Or does it assume the recipient is sitting at their desk anxious to immediately open any message from you, then carefully read it and respond in a timely manner?

This becomes even more of a problem as more and more businesspeople are checking emails on their phone while dashing between meetings. If your email is overlooked then, it may have scrolled far away by the time they return to their desk.

Decide that your job is to help that busy contact quickly make sense of any email you send.

Words That Work:
Here are five ways to make your emails stand out and get results:

1. **If you are responding to something they requested:**
   Start the subject line with, *As you requested:*

2. **If you have a question that is pivotal:**
   In subject line, put: *Important: Need to know from you*

3. **If you haven't received a response to something that's pivotal:**
   Resend the email with the identical Subject, but add, in caps, 'RESEND' as the first word on that subject line. Then in the body of the email, insert at the very top:

   (I'm resending this in case it didn't get through to you. Important action needed. Thanks, Ken)

4. **If it is a very important email,** take a few seconds and make a quick call right after sending it. Leave a very brief message:
   "Hi Bill, quick message This is Ken, I've just sent an email that needs your attention right away. If for any reason you haven't received it, please call me immediately at …. Thanks."

5. **Don't ever make your emails *High Priority* unless they truly are** – to the recipient. It really ticks people off.

135

Overreacting

In some selling situations, less is more.

Just because a problem pops up and you happen to have an arsenal at your disposal doesn't mean the best thing to do is to use it.

Let's suppose you've been working with a prospect and things have been progressing nicely. At the last minute, however, he unexpectedly questions the capabilities of one particular aspect of your solution.

You recognize the question – it's how one of your competitors tries to undermine you. You've seen this before, and your company has armed you with all sorts of facts to combat it. You're poised to let loose with that salvo.

But wait – is that what your prospect wants?

If you inundate him based on his question, you are validating the issue. Why else would you make such a big deal of it? You have just raised that competitor up to equal standing with you, despite being far ahead of them before this question came up.

Plus, your claims now put that prospect in the position of having to dig in and figure out all these competing claims before moving ahead. More work for him.

He may decide the safest thing to do is to stop everything until he gets time to sort this out.

Maybe what that prospect really wanted was comfort. Why don't you give it to them and find out?

After a pause, treat this issue as a non-issue with something along the lines of:

<u>Words That Work:</u>
"Hmm. I really don't hear that as an issue from the many companies we work with – and you know our accounts include …, … and ….

" I do know that a particular competitor of ours tries to make that accusation as a way of getting attention. If you'd like, I'll be happy to put you in touch with one of our senior engineers to discuss this area in depth. Or I can get you all sorts of data regarding this."

There. With your tone and words, you've diminished the issue, not elevated it. That just may be what your customer was hoping to hear. Now he can continue along with this purchase and get back to work, thank you.

Don't use a hammer to swat a fly. Subtle technique can often accomplish what brute force cannot.

The "Hey Jim!" Factor

A technology sale either grows or it dies. If only you and a single contact at a company know about it, your sale is vulnerable indeed.

What happens if that lone contact gets preoccupied by another project or goes on sick leave? What if he or she is reassigned or leaves the company? Your sale will likely die on the vine, with no one else at that company even knowing.

That's why getting Jim involved is so important. Jim is the person we want your contact rushing to talk to after your meeting, or better still during your meeting, as in *"Hey Jim! Come in here; you're going to like this."*

What is Jim's title? Ideally, Jim (or Jan) will be your contact's boss, or better still a business manager with budget. But even if Jim is a peer, it still means your sale is getting more exposure.

That should be the goal in every first call on a new prospect. You want the person you're meeting with to be so impressed and enthused that he can't wait to tell Jim about it.

What will accomplish that? It depends on the solution you're selling, and what will make someone a hero over there.

Here's the test to use: It's got to be big enough where Jim will say in response, *"Really! This could be great! Does Sue know about this?"* Grow sale, grow.

How Senior Executives Think

It's different at the top.

I've taught about selling to senior levels of management to sales teams at companies large and small – including IBM salespeople and reseller channels across Europe, Asia and the Americas.

You might be wondering, why would a company like IBM, who has top level relationships at every major corporation, want to invest in this? Because:

1. Senior executives are often briefly involved in lower level decisions at the final stages, and can veto them.
2. No one is born understanding the priorities of top level managers and the best ways to sell to them.

Here are some of the lessons salespeople have found most useful when the sale involves higher levels in organizations.

Let's start with why those managers are different: It's not that they're born that way – the job changes them.

Because of their scope and responsibility, they're forced to think and act in ways that are fundamentally different from the other levels of management. As many salespeople have learned the hard way, that can mean a meeting with unexpected and undesirable turns.

Since most people have never been a senior executive, let me take you into that mindset. Here are some of the ways in which they are different:

They Think Bigger: They have to. With such a large area of responsibility, they can't focus on details or day-to-day matters. That's what their subordinates are for. This means your usual talking points (and presentation), if unchanged, is likely to quickly bore them.

Senior Executives Live Slightly in the Future: They're looking out about 12-18 months. Their job is to envision the company's future and figure out how to get there. That's why they care about things with big impact.

Their Time is Short, and So is Their Attention Span: They'll interrupt, they'll challenge claims. They'll leave if they get bored. Because they can.

They Know Things Others Do Not – But Can't Talk About Them: Their job has them privy to all sorts of big things that are in the works – possible acquisitions, reorganizations, expansion into new businesses or markets, etc. Very often they know things that no one else you've been talking with is even aware of.

Their inside knowledge of upcoming plans and possible changes is one of the reasons they're getting involved.

They're stepping in, however briefly, to make sure this purchase will fit in with the future changes only they know about.

You can't, however, ask them about their as-yet-unannounced plans. Disclosing such insider information to an outsider, especially a salesperson, would be foolish – and it's probably against the law.

But as we'll see in Chapter 5, that doesn't mean you're helpless.

7 Secrets of the Very Successful Salesperson

Lots of people are in sales, and more join every year. All kinds of people, each with their own style. What I've noticed, having met and worked with so many at all stages of professional growth, is that the top achievers have certain traits in common.

The good news is that few people are born with all these characteristics. You can choose to develop and hone them and put them to work for you.

1. They Love Selling

Let's face it – some people simply dread talking to others and asking for their confidence. They mistakenly see it as bullying, not helping.

Such people simply aren't going to excel in selling. Oh, it's possible to have someone toil away doing something against their nature – in the circus they even have bears that ride bikes. But don't expect great achievement; very few bears become renowned cyclists.

So if you don't love the challenge of selling, and the thrill of making that big sale, do yourself a favor and find another field.

2. They Need a Strong Self Image

There must be an inner confidence, at least in their capacity of presenting a company's wares or services. Selling is one of the few jobs that guarantees rejection – it takes a strong belief system to deal with this every day, every week, every month.

3. They Must Like and Respect Others

We humans have an amazing ability to sense when someone is trying to help us, versus when they're trying to merely help themselves to

141

our money. The ignorant person thinks they can trick others into buying. Not for long.[*]

4. They'd Better Be Organized

Selling is all about follow-through. It doesn't matter what system is used, or whether it's formal or if much is 'kept up in their head'. But there had better be one. Otherwise, the sheer number of details guarantees problems galore.

5. They Must Know More

Today more than ever, a salesperson has to bring value to make the time spent a worthy investment. A top salesperson is really a consultant; meeting with him or her should be worth $200 in terms of ideas, insights and value gained. And one area that salesperson had better know is how people learn, absorb, and make decisions.[**]

6. They Make Things Happen

They're on the lookout. Seeing what's going in the industry, and within their territory. They're not waiting for their company to provide things. Human brochures make lousy salespeople, even though they do occasionally get lucky. My money is on the proactive salesperson; he or she will run circles around the rest.

7. They Never Stop Learning, Thinking and Growing

You're already one of them. By reading this book you show your commitment to moving ahead and knowing more. By putting it into action, you'll become ever more valuable to customers.

---

[*] Sure, we all get tricked a few times in our lives – that's how we learn what to watch out for.

[**] See Chapter 7 for more about reaching higher levels.

Chapter 5

Mastering the Meeting

In sports, it's all about what happens on game day. You can practice all week, you can have the best plays. What really matters, though, is how you perform at the actual game.

In sales, it's all about your meetings. That's where sales are won. Those interactions decide if the purchase becomes a priority.

In this section, I'll share lessons about mastering the different kinds of meetings you will attend. I'll also include best practices for handling interrupters and late arrivers, leveraging mixed meetings where participants have conflicting interests, and what to do if they get that bored look in their eyes.

In a perfect world every meeting of yours would go as planned. Of course, they rarely do. But now you will have more ways to keep the challenges that pop up from derailing your sale.

Joint Sales Calls

When you are selling a complex solution, you often bring specialists along with you. These technical folks may be brilliant, but selling is not their area of expertise.

Regardless, they may have enormous influence and credibility with your customer. What they say or don't say can make or break a sale.

That's why it is essential for you to gently educate them so they can best help that customer and your sale. Here's an approach that will avoid many problems.

Before the sales call, over a cup of coffee, say this to your technical partner:

Words That Work:
"I don't know nearly as much as you about technical things, but I do know about customers. So here are some ground rules I go by; let me know if you disagree with any of them.

- *"You are incredibly influential. Don't be surprised if they take every comment you make as gospel.*

- *"Because of this, avoid making flippant remarks about anything — they may misinterpret it. if in doubt, don't say it.*

- *"Don't insult our competitors, except in a respectful way. Start any criticism with, 'From what I've heard...'*

- *"Please, please, don't inundate businesspeople with details. They want confidence, not an education.*

- *"Steer any lengthy technical issues to the end of the meeting. Then follow my lead; I may want to turn it into a separate meeting.*

- *"Never, even in jest, say anything disparaging about our company, our products, our past products, or salespeople.*

- *"Don't talk in elevators or cafeterias. You never know who is listening."*

After the sales call, it's time for a review. Tread gently when critiquing. People can be unexpectedly sensitive about such things, especially if they wanted to impress you.

If there are any rough spots to discuss, say three nice things, then point out any areas where their comments weren't ideal. Then ask if there were things you could have done better from their point of view.

Give Them a Magic Wand

We've all been there – at meetings where things start to take a bad turn.

It might be because the prospect is getting overwhelmed with information, or distracted, or any other reason. You can sense the sale is growing more and more distant.

Before they've completely talked themselves out of everything, here's an approach that can work wonders for changing the mood:

Words That Work:
"Lee, let me ask you a question. If you had a magic wand, what would you like to see happen?"

It's a thought provoking question, designed to lift them out of their reality and visit a wonderful place in their imagination where they can make things happen. Don't be surprised if the mood immediately changes.

Lee is likely to answer, *"A magic wand? Okay, here's what I would love – if…"* Let him go on.

You just may find that your sale is back on track. I've seen it happen many times, and in addition you now have important information on what they really want from you and your solution.

Selling Senior Executives

As we discussed in 'How Senior Executives Think'[*], top executives are a different breed.

You can't use 'probing questions' with them. That's too bad, because if you could, you could cater the discussion to how your solution would help reach their goals.

Despite that, even in a short meeting there are ways to win the confidence of that senior exec and learn their real priorities.

Here's how to do it:

Step One: Show You Understand Their World
Right after the handshake and any small talk, begin this way:

Words That Work:
"Since our time is limited, what I'd like to do is briefly speak to issues that senior executives at other customers of ours have found of interest and importance as they look to the future of their business."

Bingo. Now they know that you get it and that you will be brief. Unlike so many salespeople, you understand that their interests are different from their subordinates.

If you are expected to have a formal presentation, make it very short[**] and hit only truly big topics. Don't worry about ignoring all the wonderful details; they're very good at asking questions if they so choose.

---

[*] Chapter 4

[**] Always err on the side of making it too short. This is one meeting where you don't want to get trapped by your slides (see Chapter 6 for more on this).

Step Two: Have Them Disclose Their Secret Priority
You can't ask outright, so here's how to do it: Provide three, and let them pick one. The following example will show you what I mean.

As soon as possible in your meeting, get to the point where you can say:

<u>Words That Work:</u>
"As you look to the future, to where you want your company to be in, say, 12 or 18 months, there are likely to be three areas in which we can help in a very cost-effective, leveraged way."

"What I'd like to do, if it's okay with you, is give you a very brief – under a minute – overview of three different ways we're helping companies similar to yours. Then I'll be happy to delve into any one of them with specifics if you would like."

What should those three stories be? Of course it depends on your solution, but they should be brief, easy to grasp, and of big impact.

Here's an example of those three areas from a client of mine, **Brainshark**. As way of background, you should know that their cloud-based technology lets you easily add a voice track to any PowerPoint presentation, along with powerful tracking and metrics about who has opened it, how long they spent with it, if they completed it, if they forwarded it, etc.

In their case, the three ways they're helping companies might be:

<u>Words That Work:</u>
"One of our customers, (name), is using our solution to gain greater control over their sales revenue pipeline. Instead of guessing, they now know, for certain, if emailed communications are viewed, by whom, and for how long. This has tremendous impact on accurate revenue projections and company planning, as well as on assigning resources.

"Another customer, (name), has dramatically lowered their costs of training, since now they can now create many of their training modules in-house within hours, without involving outside resources that previously took weeks and cost far more. That has had great impact in many ways, including on their expanding their channel.

"Lastly, if you'd like I can tell you about another customer, (name), who has reduced the cost of their annual sales meeting by over a million dollars because salespeople, before traveling to the event, now learn the marketing and new product information. This previously took up days in face-to-face presenting in hotel rooms. Now they spend fewer days away from selling; that million-dollar savings was just one of many ways it had impact.

"Of course, I can only tell you public information* about those companies, but I think you will get ideas you can use. Which of those three would you like to hear about?"

You've just brought a lot of value in a very short amount of time.

More importantly, as that executive tells you which of the three they'd like to know more about, you now know where their interests lie. That's powerful knowledge. Plus, you've also just exposed them to benefits in areas which they may not been considering.

Senior executives have the same driving forces that all people in business have. By knowing helpful ways to gain insight into their dreams and priorities, you can become a trusted resources to them.

---

* This is an important phrase – you want that executive to know that you won't be telling their inside information to anyone once they become a customer.

Mixed Meetings, Meet the Players

If your sales is moving ahead, time will come for the mixed meeting.

The good news is that all the right people will be in the room: Business executive, Mid-level day-to-day person, and Technical evaluator. All have their role if this sale is to happen.

The bad news? Each has different interests and priorities. Somehow, you need to speak to these disparate mindsets and have each of the players conclude that you respect, understand, and would bring value to their world.

Let's look at each, then how to satisfy all of them at the same time.

Captain Industry:
That's our name for the business executive in the room. Time with this person is the hardest to get. They can get up and leave any time they're bored or feel the discussion doesn't need them. This possible purchase is but one of many things on their plate; easily pushed away if it fails to excite them or seems marginal in impact.

We may not know much about them personally or their priorities, but we can be sure:

1. They know less and care less about technical matters than you or the others in the room.

2. They are privy to things the others know nothing about, such as upcoming unannounced changes.

3. They're likely to be much more attuned to the world beyond the walls of that company – competitors, industry trends, wants of their biggest customers, etc.

Harry/Harriet, the Harried Day-to-Day Person
While the Captain looks at things from a strategic viewpoint on high, Harriet's job has her living in the moment. She deals with daily business life and the headaches that come with it.

She may be your direct contact, but even if she's not, you've met with Harriet before and have some level of relationship. She's the one who made this meeting happen. You and your solution have impressed her enough to make her want to stick her neck out to request that the Captain spend time here.

One big variable is the dynamic between Harriet and the Captain. Depending on that corporate culture and the personalities involved, her influence may be large or small. In a moment we will explore how to find out about this.

Conan the Evaluator
He or she knows technology, is proud of that knowledge, and may see their job as protecting the company from fast-talking salespeople.

Here's something to keep in mind: Conan rarely is in meetings with the Captain and may see this as a chance to impress him even if this is at your expense.[*]

[*] See 'Technical Interrupters'

Mixed Meetings, Setting It Up

Meeting with Captain Industry, Harried Harriet and Conan the Evaluator[*] can be challenging. Here are some specific ways to ensure a positive outcome.

Long Before the Meeting Begins
As soon as the possibility of this meeting comes up, ask Harriet:

<u>Words That Work:</u>
"What do you think will be most valuable for the Captain to see and hear in this meeting? I want to make sure it is on-target for his interests and attention span – given your experience, what would be best?"

This immediately tells her that you are attuned to meeting with such executives. That's good; it will probably increase the chances of that meeting happening.

If at all possible, pose that question over the phone or in person – not via email. In conversation, Harriet may tell you about their history, what's worked best in other meetings, and what to avoid. You won't get the same detail or candor in an email. Then ask:

<u>Words That Work:</u>
"Can you tell me about the others who will be in the meeting?"

When she does, ask about their priorities. This is comforting to Harriet. It's clear you know what you're doing and won't be an embarrassment.

When she mentions the technical people expected to be there, ask:

---

[*] See previous section.

Words That Work:
"What should I know about them? Sometimes they can try to show off by putting the vendor on the spot with questions that will only bore the executive. Think that's a problem here, or not really?"

This makes it easy for her to let you know and helps in a second way. If she hears herself saying, *"Well, Conan can be tough.",* then she will be more likely to respond to your next question:

Words That Work:
"Think it might be a good idea for me to speak or meet with him beforehand?"

If she says yes, she'll help arrange that and you will be able to befriend or at least declaw Conan before that fateful big meeting.

At the Meeting, Play to the Captain...
Engage and impress him and the sale advances. Fail to do this and all bets are off.

Lead with big strategic and competitive benefits of your solution. Don't only speak to savings. Bring ideas that can make the Captain look visionary and be a hero.

...But Include All
They want to show their value, too. If it seems that you only care about the Captain, the others will feel ignored and demand attention in ways that may not be helpful.

To include all, combine each executive level benefit with benefits that affect each of the others. All you need to do this is to add a sentence or two for each constituency.

The way to do that is to start with something focused on the Captain, then shift to each other person. Here's an example:

Words That Work:

"We brought a similar solution to ...., a company of your size but in another industry. [*] *To Lee Smith, the senior executive over there, it brought... (high level benefit). By the way, if you'd like, I can arrange a phone conversation between you and Lee.*

"In terms of day-to-day business, however, as I've discussed with Harriet, it changed ... and reduced costs of ...

"As for the technical side of implementation over there, their IT team will tell you we brought it in on time and on budget, and, as I've discussed with Conan, it actually streamlined ... "

Follow this approach for each example you bring up and watch how it pleases everybody.

---

[*] If you start with an example in their industry, they may get distracted by thinking about competitors, or by wondering if you will share their details with those companies.

Technical Interrupters

"Well before you go into that, can I ask how this will work if we're streaming via the Hubble telescope on a Tuesday during a solar eclipse?"

You're selling in a mixed meeting – and suddenly one of the technical people is interrupting your flow with a complicated question that is not at all critical to the discussion. Whether it's because they're being impulsive or are trying to show off, this presents a problem for you.

You know the answer, but it's not a short one. If you delve in now it will surely bore the others. It will also reward the interrupter and probably encourage him to interrupt again. What do you do?

Words That Work:
"Phil, the short answer is, yes, we definitely can do that. In fact, right this minute, at accounts like ...., ..., and ... they are using our solution to do precisely that.

"But can I ask that we delve into this either after this meeting or at a separate one? That way we can cover our agenda without going over. Is that okay?"

Important: Before you say another word, wait for Phil to nod or say, *"Yes."* If you don't, he may feel he's being bullied or trivialized in front of others. By a salesperson, no less. By asking so respectfully, after your very logical reason, you defuse this potential problem.

Your brief comment, by the way, didn't only avoid having the group endure a detailed answer. It also quickly answered that, yes, you certainly can do that. You even named companies who are doing it right now, subtly reminding everyone that you have happy customers all over.

To Prevent Technical Interruptions:

That was how to handle Phil *in the middle of a meeting*. The best approach is to prevent this from happening in the first place. To do that, take 20 seconds to start your meeting with:

<u>Words That Work:</u>

"As I'm sure you know, we could talk for hours on this. But our time is limited today, and to make this as valuable as possible to all of you, can I suggest we save in-depth technical questions for after the meeting, or for their own meeting? That way we can cover our agenda and give those questions the time they deserve. Is that okay?"*

Pause for a beat, and then move on. If anyone balks, don't fight. With a smile, simply say you just want to make sure the meeting doesn't run late, but you will be happy to answer any questions. Despite their posturing, that person will nevertheless think twice before forcing all on a techie detour. Mission accomplished.

After the meeting, if you feel Phil is a sensitive type, privately mention to him that you hope you didn't seem out of place and your only intent was to make sure others didn't complain later if you had not had time to cover everything. He will probably appreciate this extra attention.

---

* If you haven't already confirmed, this would be a good time to make sure just how much time you have. "Am I correct that we have an hour?" The key player may answer, "Well, that was the plan, but I have to leave in about 25 minutes." Now you know, and can adjust your flow accordingly.

"Price Please?" Interrupters

"Before you go any further, what's this going to cost?"

This may be a problem – they're asking about price before you have a chance to convey the value or likely return on that investment.[*]

There are two very different reasons this question gets posed. In some cases they're just curious; they want to understand roughly how big or small this deal is as they listen to you. In other situations, the questioner is challenging. Let' look at each case.

Just Curious: Sometimes that person simply wants to know a ballpark figure. So establish a range, making it as wide and contingent as your business requires – then move on. For example:

Words That Work:
"The entry point is about $30,000, and I'd guess that for a business of your size it would range from $40-75,000, depending on a number of variables we would have to discuss."

Quickly follow with, *"For that sort of investment, you should expect to see what our other customers see: A revenue impact of between $200,000 - $400,000 within the first year."*

Rule: Never end a discussion of price with a number of what it will cost – it kills the conversation. Instead, continue on to include the payback that investment is likely to bring – a far better topic for them to now ask about.

---

[*] No doubt you've qualified the opportunity beforehand – this is often asked by an executive who is only now joining in the discussion.

By establishing a range and much larger payback number, you will now hear if that minimum price was out of their ballpark. If you don't, assume it's affordable and continue on.

The Challenger: There will be times when you sense that if you give the price at this moment – before conveying the value – it will ruin your chances of going any further. This is a delicate moment.

In such situations, here's a phrase I love – but it has to be delivered with a smile and followed up quickly:

Words That Work:
"Cost? Oh, if this isn't right for you, then there is no cost."

Which is absolutely correct – if they decide it's wrong for them, there will be no purchase. But now you have to quickly intrigue them so they will postpone pricing matters for a few minutes as you convey value and create desire:

"I can assure you that – if it is right for your company – the investment will make sense and even be a bargain. Otherwise companies like (name four customers) wouldn't have chosen us."

Logical and intriguing; you now have them wondering what others have seen. Now you have to ask for a little time:

Words That Work:
"What I would like to ask is that you grant me three or four minutes to explain our value before going into pricing. My thinking is that if you don't see the value, talking price would just be a waste of your time anyway. Is that okay?"

Wait for their okay before saying another word. If they are a reasonable person, you'll get it. If they balk at this logical and sensible request, well you now know to crank up the cost-benefit analysis, and even then, don't expect much here.

"How Much Longer?" Interrupters

You're in the middle of your presentation and you hear this. It's time to make a quick determination; it shouldn't be hard to do.

Are they asking because they're fascinated and want to be sure they have enough time? If that's the case, simply tell them how much time you will need to complete your presentation.

Or are they asking because they've grown bored with your slides or formal presentation? All is lost unless you fix this right now. Bored people rarely buy.[*]

It won't be enough to go faster; they've already given up on your presentation. It's time for to do something dramatic if you have any hope of regaining their interest.

Words That Work:

"You know, let's turn off the slides[**]. Let's see if anything I've talked about, or that we're doing at companies like yours, is of interest to you."

Close your computer and move to the whiteboard. Write down three customer names, nice and big. Then give three quick examples – meaning 30 seconds each – of what your solution is accomplishing for each of them.

Ask if they find any of those examples intriguing and relevant to their goals at their company. If they say yes, congratulations. Now you

---

[*] You don't need to wait to hear the question – anytime a key person looks at his or her watch it's time to make sure they're engaged.

[**] Or, "Let's forget my formal presentation." if you're not using slides.

have a chance at rekindling their interest and a conversation. Proceed as you see fit — as long as it doesn't include going back to the presentation that bored them.

If they say no, ask an open-ended question, *"What sort of impact are you folks looking for?"* You will either hear a response you can work with, or one that tells you there is no chance here.

Either way, you may want to ask the following before leaving:

"Can I ask you a question? I'd like to have this presentation reworked so it's more valuable to people like you. What would you suggest I tell the people back at my office?"

Then bring that feedback to the powers that be and get a better presentation. No one in your company's upper management wants to waste money fielding salespeople just so prospects can become bored.

Late Arrivers

"Sorry I'm late. Just continue; I'll catch on."

Uh-oh. You've got a problem. It's the key executive, finally showing up. His or her interest will either make or break this sale.

In all likelihood, you and everyone else waited for that person, then you were told to begin without them. Now you're 10 or 15 minutes into your presentation.

What do you do?

Clearly you can't go back and start from the beginning. If you "just continue", however, there's no way he or she will catch up. More likely, they'll get confused and bored and simply leave. Opportunity lost.

Take this tack and help everyone:

Words That Work:
 "Let me just take 30 seconds to summarize what we've covered. Then if you want details on any part, just let me know."

Then give a lightning fast summary, along the lines of:
"We briefly looked at the three reasons why our product has been so successful at companies of your size (list them quickly, without details). We had an overview of our support system and how it reduces your costs and risk. And now we're in the middle of what a typical installation involves, and about to show how soon you're likely to see a competitive advantage.

(To rest of group) "Is that about right, or did I leave anything out?"

You have just accomplished so much:

- You've brought that executive up to speed, in an easy to remember, big picture way.

- You've reminded the others of what they've just seen, again reinforcing in an easy to remember way.

- You've intrigued everyone about what's coming next.

All while being totally professional in a situation in which many would have withered.

Not bad for 30 seconds.

Why the question to the group?   Two reasons:

1. It gives them a chance to amplify any of your points based upon their knowledge of what's most important to that executive.
2. Even if the reply is merely a consensus "Yes", it tells the executive that everyone is on board with the short summary you just gave.

Chapter 6

It's All in the Presentation

You've worked long and hard to arrange this presentation. Stakes are high; the people you're meeting with will either advance your sale or block it. That's why presenting is such a critical selling skill.

That's true in any business, but the challenge is greater when selling technology solutions. Things can get complex and confusing – and we all know that bored people rarely become customers.

With that in mind, I created my Winning Presentations seminar and workshops. It was specifically designed for technology salespeople, and I have taught it at companies ranging from startups to IBM and Accenture.

This section brings techniques you can use every time you present, and even includes specific advice for presenting to large groups or in international settings.

It has some surprising insights – such as why you should *never* ask for questions at the very end. Get ready to have a newfound advantage the next time the spotlight is on you.

How to Present Brilliantly

There are many books about presenting and I think I've read just about all of them at least once. I'll bet you've read a few of them, too.

Advice ranges from 'Say interesting things' to 'Visualize them naked'.[*]

When it comes to selling technology solutions, I've found that two of the most important rules for being an outstanding presenter are simply these:

1. **Say More Than You Show**

2. **Know More Than You Say**

[*] No thanks.

PowerPoint: Friend or Foe?

Here's a humbling thought: Salespeople have a very limited toolkit. Knowledge and Words. You and your competitors both have knowledge and you both have words.

But there is a third tool. It's the tool that multiplies your ability to get your message into the minds of others. It's called presentation software and the most common one today is PowerPoint.

Countless articles have been written griping about boring slideshows, but the fact remains that visuals have impact.

Studies repeatedly show that a person using visuals will have greater impact over one who merely talks. [*]

It makes sense. Visuals, if used correctly, engage more of our minds and also prevent daydreaming. The person who does that will connect better with the audience than one who doesn't.

That's why I have an assignment for you, one that will lead to more sales and be worth literally tens of thousands of dollars to you over the course of your career: Decide to learn and become masterful with PowerPoint (or whatever presentation software you choose).

Do it in small bites. Carve out 15 minutes a day and start with the basics. Within two weeks you will be amazed at how much you can

[*] The most quoted one is the 1981 Wharton School Study; it showed that using visuals not only improves communication effectiveness, but interestingly, also *the audience's perception of the presenter*. Yes, people will think you're smarter and better at your job when you effectively use visuals. They may even buy sooner.

now do. Soon you will be able to easily customize a presentation in meaningful ways or create a compelling leave-behind.

With this newfound ability, you will now be able to make a stronger impression on or after every sales call. I guarantee you will see results even just from being able to provide a tailored leave-behind – it will travel and help your contact expand the sale while underscoring your professionalism.

In a sense, you will soon have a super-power in selling. One that makes you more valuable to customers and shortens your sales cycles. One that helps you make more money.

Not only will you have an advantage over competing salespeople, but you will also have an advantage over the old you. That's an upgrade that will continue to pay dividends throughout your career.

Opening Strong

Your First Slide Speaks Volumes
You've sat through plenty of presentations; you know that people make sweeping judgments early on – starting with the title slide.

Think about the presentation you usually give. At the first moment, when absolutely everyone is paying attention, what does your title slide say?

Is it about you – dominated by your company's logo with a title that merely names what you will be talking about? Opportunity lost.

Far better to intrigue with that first slide. Tell them this will be about them and their world. Refer to how others are benefitting because of that product or service. By using a title and subtitle, you can accomplish a lot in very few words – together they can set the tone and draw everyone in. Your first slide is an opportunity not to be ignored.

What's the Best Way to Open?
With a question. Questions are remarkably powerful – they get people thinking, they can open minds. Because they engage the viewer's mind, it is impossible for a good question to be boring.

The best ones speak to that customer's world and goals. Here's a quick example:

Ken Wax & Associates **Our Capabilities and Advantages**	or	**How Can Any Technology Salesperson Sell More – Starting Next Week?** Ken Wax & Associates

Which of these slides is more likely to pull you in to the presentation?

If you are in charge of your company's sales team – or even if you personally just want to earn more money – that slide on the right is far more compelling. That's why the right question is irresistible – it pulls people in because they want it answered.

Next, Quickly Tell Me Where We're Headed

Your first slide's job was to engage and intrigue. Now it's time to tell everyone what to expect. Have some form of agenda slide so you can quickly give an idea of what you will and won't cover, how long it will take, and your goals for this meeting.

Keep it short, and hopefully intriguing. As you quickly mention the sections areas you will cover, create desire and anticipation, as in:

Words That Work:
"And we'll look at some interesting parts of this area, including what one company found that surprised them."

Don't Overlook Telling Me Why It's Important

Either before or immediately after that agenda slide, have a slide that lets you speak to why this entire topic and presentation is so relevant and useful to this company's work. Don't expect them to intuitively know this; the people you're meeting with have a lot of other things on their minds.

Words That Work:
Don't get fancy here – it is very effective to simply have a blank slide with text in the middle that says, *"Why Is This So Important?"*

Then, with all eyes on you, briefly you tell them why and then flow into the rest of your slides.

Talking Points

They Can't Learn As Fast as You Can Talk

Time passes differently for you than for the people listening to you. You are going to be tempted to go fast, since you have so much to cover and don't want anyone to get bored.

Resist. Give people the time they need to absorb your current point before beginning the next one. If you rush, they will get overwhelmed and tune out.[*]

If your presentation has several sections, pause after each and ask if there are questions or areas they'd like to know more about. If nothing else, this gives everyone a moment to digest all you served up so they can get ready to learn more.

"Um, er, uh, um"

They're called 'placeholders' – those sounds people make when considering the best way of phrasing their next point. Those "um"s and "er"s are very distracting; brief silence is far better.

It's a common habit[**], but fortunately it is easy to stop – all you have to do is just start being aware of it. One way to do that is to place a small, easy to see note where only you can see it that says 'UM'. (Even if anyone does spot it, they won't have any idea what it means.)

---

[*] See 'How People Absorb – Or Not', Chapter 1.

[**] Interestingly, the more one knows, the greater the likelihood of using "um"s and "er"s. That's because such a person has so many mental choices about what to say next on the topic. Nevertheless, it's no badge of honor – I've known executives who were so distracting that at company events employees would keep count (which meant they weren't listening to the content, of course).

Death by Bullets

Bullet slides hurt — people quickly tire of them, and they treat all points as equals. Learn when and when not to use bullets, and whenever you do use them:

Make Each Short
They should not be full sentences. Think: headlines. Then you bring value by making that brief headline come alive.

When watching a presentation, people find it very difficult to read sentences. They quickly grow bored and tune out. If you keep the bullet point very short, they stay engaged to find out what it's all about.

Always Build
That's what it's called when the slide starts with only the first bullet point visible, and the next one doesn't arrive until you click for it.[*]

This is surprisingly important to do — otherwise as soon as your slide appears your audience will begin reading all of those bullet points. While they're doing that, they're certainly not listening to you.

Even worse, once they're done reading, why listen to you rehash points they already think they well know?

Don't Read for Them
The people you're meeting with already know how to read; doing this brings no value and is very annoying. Instead of reading, use phrases that are different from the slide and bring value with additional information.

---

[*] Yes, this does mean more clicking per slide. See 'Presenting in Big Rooms' for information on the benefits of having a wireless clicker.

----

11 x 6 = 66

"I've got a short slideshow for you today; it's only 11 slides!"

That may be true, but if you have six bullet points on each of those slides, you're serving up dozens and dozens of items. Do you really think anyone is going to remember them all?

No More Than Two Bullet Slides in a Row

Here's why: Because bullet slides are filled with text, they all look alike. They also demand a lot of attention, because they have so many points on them. This makes them very tiring for audiences.

If you don't break things up, they will soon tune out. So after two bullet slides, show a slide that is visually different. It can be a quote, a chart, a graph, a photo – anything that is not a virtually identical text-heavy bullet slide.

Common Mistakes to Avoid

Don't Bury Key Information
If it's important, it gets its own slide.

Want to make sure everyone pays attention to a key point? There's nothing stronger than a slide which has very few words in the center and nothing else. Now everyone focuses on you to find out why it's worth that much attention.

What if you need to provide detailed information about that key point? No problem. Following that attention-focusing slide, have a bullet slide right after which has the identical title. You make your big point, and then click to the supporting bullet slide.

Spinning Globes Change Nothing
Content is king. I'm not saying appearance doesn't matter; it does (it reflects poorly if you have an amateurish looking presentation). But content counts a lot more.

If you've got a self-centered or meandering slideshow, all the flying text and carnival graphics in the world won't save it. 'Compelling' comes from within, not as a pasted-on afterthought.

They Want a Steak, Not a Whole Cow
Your solution may do a thousand things and you may be proud of each one of them. Fine. Now pick out the most important ones and make them sizzle.

EOTAP
Easy-On-The-Acronyms-Please. They rarely help keep attention and almost guarantee your contact won't bring you to meet with business executives.

"I know you can't read this, but…"

How many times have you seen someone present a slide while acknowledging it is unreadable?

Never do this. Make that slide readable, even if it means turning that one slide into three. Better yet, keep it to one slide by figuring out what's really important and getting rid of the rest.

Here's a low tech tip for making sure a slide can be read by the everyone in the room: Print the slide out a sheet of 8½ x 11 paper. Now place that page on the floor between your feet. Look down; if you can read it without bending over, everyone in the room will be able to read it when it's up on the screen.

Click, Pause

Don't say anything important right after changing slides.

Why not? At that moment, everyone is busy reading or trying to understand that diagram. Wait a few seconds before saying anything important; otherwise what you say will be missed by many people because their attention was elsewhere.

Enhancing Any Presentation

Tell It in a Story

Facts and claims quickly grow boring, but stories appeal to our curiosity and get people involved. They're easy to remember and easy for others to retell. When the presenter says, *"Let me tell you a story..."* the audience perks up.[*]

Power of Backdrop Slide

If you want everyone's attention, put up a very short 'billboard' slide – or write one or two words on the whiteboard. Now there's no reading to be done; all eyes will be on you.

This is perfect if you're going to tell a story; if you have a busy slide up there instead you've created your own distraction.

Create Something While They're Watching

If the situation allows it, this is a very powerful technique. In addition to clicking through your slides, at a logical point, go to the easel or whiteboard to draw a diagram or emphasize a point.

For example, in my seminars when I teach 'Stuck On the Sales Ladder'[**] , I will quickly draw two ladders on the easel (one of them with some rungs missing). It not only focuses everyone's attention, but that drawing lives on after the slides are gone.

---

[*] See 'Let Me Tell You a Story' in Chapter 4 for more on why having good business stories can be like having a super power in selling.

[**] See Chapter 3 to learn why it's so important to have the right number of rungs for each prospect.

Never Have Q&A at the Very End

Never, ever, ever ask for questions at the very end[*].

I know, I know. All your business life you've seen people end by asking for questions; you may have thought it's the law. It's not – get ready for a simple ahah! that has changed thousands of salespeople forever.

If you ask for questions at the very end, the lasting memory is out of your control.

- A tough or unfair question can undo all you've done and leave everyone with a bad lasting impression.

- If there are no questions, their most vivid memory will be of you shrugging *"No? No questions? Well, ok, we're done."*

- If there are questions, people will begin leaving while you are giving answers – especially those influential ones you really wanted to talk with afterwards.

Far better to do it this way:

At the very end, your presentation should have one or two wrap-up slides. They can summarize your presentation, have a parting thought or story – whatever makes sense.

Right before them, have a backdrop slide that simply says, nice and big in the middle: **Questions? Comments?**

---

[*] Even if you only adopt this one piece of advice, you just got your money's worth from this book – and send me an email when it saves you from ending an important presentation with a troublemaker's question.

When that slide arrives, say:

Words That Work:
"Before my two final wrap-up slides, we have a little time if there are any questions or comments."

Pause for a beat or two, then if no one speaks up, click on. Do not beg for questions.

If there are questions, in most cases you will want to end the Q&A after three of them. (That's why you used the phrase *"a little time".)* If you don't do this, watch the key people leave the room.

Words That Work:
"In the interest of keeping on schedule, how about if we move on to the wrap up?"

You're not looking for an answer; click to the next slide and begin your wrap-up. Don't worry, the truly pressing questions will find you afterwards. What if a too-technical question is asked?

Words That Work:
"Is it okay if we cover that without the whole group?"

The group will love you.

Once the Q&A is behind you, deliver a compelling close to your presentation and it's time to chat with the key decision makers.

(And if an undesirable question was asked during Q&A, use this closing section to put it in perspective and remind everyone of all the important points that far outweigh it.[*])

---

[*] That's why following this rule is particularly important with a large group — otherwise so many people will have their lasting impression come from that troublesome question.

Last Words

Have a Powerful Ending
Too often, the salesperson ends with, *"And that's the end of my slides."* Then the people, and the opportunity, drift away.

You want the audience to remember the key points of your message, not an awkward non-ending.

Have a compelling ending that reminds them how important this is and the impact of their decision – even if it is just a single slide and you only take 20 seconds to articulate that thought.

Have a Duplicate of Your Final Slide
It only takes a second. Simply have your presentation software duplicate that final slide, so at the very end there are two of them, identical.

Here's why: In many cases important conversations between you and the group will take place while that final slide is up there. This is good.

But that moment is shattered if an accidental touch of the mouse has PowerPoint closing your slideshow. By having that duplicate slide, should an inadvertent click happen, nothing changes and discussion goes on uninterrupted.

After the Presentation

What About Handouts?

It's usually a good idea to leave something tangible. But what?

The easiest thing to do is print out your slides, but resist. It won't distill your key points, nor does it provide the interesting examples and details you brought up when speaking. Rarely – and I mean very rarely – will anyone slog through it. Opportunity lost.

Instead, create a handout specifically for the purpose of motivating people after the event.* Not every slide, just pick out the few that really matter. Add things that will amplify some key points, such as a reprint, customer story or excerpt from your website.

Sure, it will require more thought and effort to create such a useful tool for them. That's why your customer will notice.

Hand Out When?

I once sat in on a very high level executive presentation to 20 people in which not a single one of them heard the complete presentation. The culprit was a proud presenter, who had brought a just-published issue of *Forbes* magazine that favorably profiled their company.

He had just picked up the issue that morning. Just before beginning his presentation, he mentioned it and handed the article to the person to his right at the conference table so he could give it a quick look. That person leafed through it for a minute or so, then passed it on to the next person, who did the same. Every person in the room missed a different part of the presentation.

The lesson here: Don't create your own distractions.

* See 'PowerPoint: Friend or Foe'

The best approach is to mention at the beginning that you will be giving out a summary-handout at the end. Even if asked, resist the temptation to give it out before.[*] If you do, people will leaf ahead, then think they now know everything you will be saying – and will be far more likely to tune out or leave.

Handouts From Afar

For webinars and video conferences, provide your handouts at the end. If someone else is in charge of this, give specific instructions in your email to them when sending that file:

"Please DO NOT DISTRIBUTE THIS UNTIL AFTER the video conference. (It's much stronger when ideas arrive fresh, and providing notes before the event would undermine that impact.)"

Elevating to the Next Audience

If your goal is to get a meeting with managers or other divisions, don't be shy about it. As you begin your talk, explain how it is for this group, but that you also have a less technical shorter one that is tailored to what business executives care about.

This sets you up to ask, at the end, if the group thinks managers would want this exact presentation or the shorter one. Either answer is fine, of course – what matters is that you are now discussing elevating this.

Following Up

It's always a good idea to remind people. Figure out something you can send your contacts afterwards that *adds* to what they experienced. Do this while things are still fresh in their mind. Your goal here: Having them share this with others to expand the sale internally.

---

[*] Simply say, with a smile, "Oh, I've learned it's a mistake to create my own distraction; I hope that's okay with everyone. Please feel free to jot down your own notes; my handout will be a summary, not the complete slideshow."

The "Who Cares?" Test

Here's the test to use whenever you are reviewing a new presentation.

It may seem harsh to the well-intentioned folks who tried to fit in so much, but it poses the question every prospect will ask.

For every item on every slide, ask: *"Who will care about this?"*

If the answer is, *"Well, this is important for them to know."* it's time to stop and examine that slide. Says who? Will that busy, distracted prospect see any reason to pay attention to this? What's in it for *them*?

If the prospect doesn't care, they will tune out. So would you. Either delete that slide or rewrite it so it connects with that prospect's world.

Trapped By Your Company's Slides

In my seminars, salespeople often ask, *"What can I do if my company's slideshow is so long and boring?"*

My answer is always, you can overcome this as long as *you're* not boring. Such slideshows, however, do make selling more difficult.

The problem is that long slideshows trap the salesperson. If the slide is there, you can't ignore it. Each point must be mentioned, if only briefly. That can be a meeting-killer when the customer's eyes have glazed over and you still have a dozen slides to go.

Often the people inside your company who create the presentations don't realize this. You may be able to teach them by asking, for every new slideshow, *"What do you suggest we do if customers don't want to – or can't – sit through all these slides and bullets?"*

What can you do in the meantime?

If your company doesn't have a policy forbidding it (some large companies do, in the name of consistency)[*], you might want to make your own very brief version of that too-heavy slideshow. The easiest way to do that is to remove almost everything from each slide except the key message and a single supporting item. Place both in the center of the slide, with plenty of white space all around.

Now you have a background for each of those topics. You can go as quickly or slowly as your customer wants. Need to show a diagram? Use the white board or a sheet of plain paper on the desk – you will

---

[*] If you can't change your company's slideshow, see 'How Much Longer Interrupters' in Chapter 5 for another approach.

find it has far more impact when you create it, as opposed to clicking to it. More memorable, too (they'll keep that sheet of paper).

By reducing the number of slides (especially bullet slides), you give yourself the ability to adapt to the audience or to sudden changes in allotted time. You can still speak to whatever topics you please; but now you're in control.

When Equipment Fails

It's every salesperson's nightmare. It has happened to me, it's either happened to you or it will.

After months of effort, you finally have a big sales presentation with all the right people in the room. But disaster strikes. Maybe it's that your computer won't work. Or their projector won't synch up with it – or the one they have breaks. A common problem is when you need an internet connection but it's running erratically or not at all.

When things go wrong, it needn't mean disaster. If you are prepared it can actually enhance the impression you make. You can often emerge better off than if the equipment had worked fine.

This was driven home to me a few years back, when the beginning of a presentation literally blew up in my face.

It was speaking at an IBM division's annual channel partner conference in Orlando; I was returning for the fifth year as a featured speaker and the audience was well over 1,000 people. Mine was the first talk of the day and I planned to wake everyone up by starting with a quick magic trick.

To make a point about customers and their expectations, I would walk on, slowly blow up a large clear balloon and then dramatically pierce it with a foot-long needle (suffice it to say, despite expectations, it was not going to pop). From there, we would flow into my talk.

All was going well as I blew up the balloon, each breath building anticipation for what I will do next. But then, as I'm tying the balloon, it popped. Everyone laughs and I sure have their attention – what does a 'master presenter' do when things go awry?

If I take the time to blow up another balloon, that little trick becomes too time consuming and too much the focus of attention. Do I just dive into my talk despite that failed start?

I paused a beat, looked at the audience for a moment as if to say, now what do I do? Then I reached inside the podium and brought out an already-inflated backup balloon that I had placed there earlier just in case anything went wrong.[*]

The applause was deafening. I smiled, did the little trick, made my point, and added another point about being prepared for the unexpected when in important presentations. Session saved, even enhanced.

In day-to-day selling, the problem won't be low-tech balloons; it will be a computer, a projector, or the internet connection.

Suddenly, Your Audience is Now Rooting for You
Before we go into specifics for each situation, let's consider what is going through the minds of the people in your meeting when a technical problem befalls the presenter.

Each person is thinking:

> 1) I sure am glad this isn't happening to *me*.

> 2) Let's see how he (or she) handles it.

That first thought is huge – don't ever forget it. They are actually identifying with you and rooting for your success because if the situation was reversed, they'd sure want to have things work out for them.

---

[*] Believe it or not, I also had a *second* blown-up balloon under there. I don't like to take chances.

Turning this into a success depends on how you've planned and prepared, and what you say in the moment. Let's look at each of these specific situations.

Computer Failure:
For any important presentation, arrive with a thumb drive in your pocket that has the presentation on it. It will be very impressive that you can reach in a pocket, hand the USB drive to someone and continue your talk as they get a replacement computer up and running.

To be safe, have your presentation in three formats:

- PowerPoint (assuming that's your presentation software)

- PowerPoint Show (which can run on computers that do not have PowerPoint installed, or have an old version)

- Adobe PDF (as a last resort – it can be shown on almost anything)

That way, no matter what substitute computer is found, your show can go on.

Words That Work:
In a confident voice, *"We seem to be having a computer problem. I've brought a USB drive with the slides; let's see if we can get this working in the next 2 or 3 minutes. If we can't, I'll continue on, but you'll get just me, without PowerPoint."*

Everyone now know what's going on, that any delay will be a short one (so not to leave), and what will happen even if no computer can be made to work. They also know that you are a professional who has clearly planned well.

Projector Failure:

This is almost the same problem, except that finding and powering up a replacement is a bigger ordeal and takes more time. Make a similar announcement, but be prepared to do the first few minutes without slides, so you can begin even as they are setting up the replacement unit.

If it turns out no projector will be available, you have to be ready to make your key points without slides. Always have a print-out of your presentation with you, as a memory aid.

Words That Work:

"We may not have visuals, but that's okay. The four key points I think you will find most valuable will come across even without PowerPoint."

Internet Failure

A slow connection can be as bad as complete loss of connection. Slow loading pages can bore everyone; be ready to switch to your emergency plan

This one is surprisingly easy to prepare for, but it does require a bit of time A day or two before your presentation, in a setting where the internet is fine, run through the web part of your presentation. As you do this, take screen shots of each webpage as it comes up.

Then create a separate slideshow of those screen shots. Should you need to give up on the internet, simply click into that screenshot presentation. Have that file on your computer and your USB drive.

Words That Work:

"We're having a problem with the internet and it looks like it won't be quickly solved, so I'll use screen shots I captured earlier this week just in case of such a problem."

Then switch to that screen-capture slideshow and continue on without further apology. They will easily grasp what would have been served up if the internet was working; the show will go on.

Don't ever worry about technical problems; simply arrive ready. Such preparedness and poise will speak volumes about both you and your company – and if anything goes wrong, the people in your meeting will probably hold you in even higher regard because of your forethought.

Presenting in Big Rooms

I've given many keynotes for corporations where the audience was over 1,000 people – but even presenting to 30 or 50 people has its special challenges. The room itself can present problems, plus your audience will likely include people with varying interests and priorities.

In my experience, once the presentation begins, the number of people there shouldn't matter. You are only presenting to one person, anyway – at least that is how each person should feel, that you are talking directly to them.

Group presentations can be won or lost even before a single slide is shown. Here are some tips for maximizing your success:

Ask to See the Room in Advance
It's always good to know what to expect; doing this will make you more comfortable leading up to the event.

Get There Early
Plug everything in and make sure there are no problems. Do this early enough so there's time for a solution to be found. If there are people there handling the AV, meet them and make them your friends.

Don't Show Slides Before the Show
You will want to run through your slides, but not in a way that early arrivers get to see them. Know your equipment and how to toggle the signal so it only shows on your machine and not the external projector. Worst case, go low tech: Lean a sheet of paper over the projector's lens while you do that review.

Bring a Mouse or Remote Clicker

Otherwise, you are tethered to your notebook or must return to it every time you change a slide. It is far more professional if you don't have to hover like that. Even in a smaller room, using an ordinary mouse gives you some freedom – plus it will be much easier to find the button and click while talking, as opposed to obviously looking for the much smaller one on your notebook each time.

If There's a Microphone, Use It

I've seen confident salespeople say, *"Oh, I don't need that!"*

Yes, you do. That's why they have one. In larger rooms, sound bounces off the walls; very often people in the middle and back will not hear things clearly unless you're using the audio system.

If You Can, Get a Clip-on Microphone

That will allow you to move around, which is much better than being stuck behind the podium the entire time. Ask beforehand if they have one, and when you arrive make sure it's there. Do a sound check early, before people arrive.* (By the way, if you need to cough or sneeze while wearing a lapel mic, place your hand over it and look the other way. Otherwise it will be startlingly loud.)

Have a Printout of Your Slides Nearby

Useful for a last minute review, and can be a lifesaver if your technology fails and you need to speak without slides.

Meet the Early Arrivers

Don't be shy, take 10 seconds to walk over, introduce yourself and shake hands, and maybe ask a few questions. It's always good to have friends in the room; now you do.

---

* If you're wearing a wireless lapel mic, be very attuned to when it is on. Any comment you make may be broadcast to all, or at least to the AV crew. That may include your trip to the restroom. Oh yes, it does happen.

Before Starting, Shake Hands with Your Audience

Not literally, of course – but it is important to take a moment to connect before diving in. People in your audience want to know that you are aware of them as people. Equally importantly, you may want to use this opportunity to learn about the audience.

For example, at my keynote for **Progress Software**'s Annual User Group conference, there were over 1500 people in the room. But who were they? All technical-users, or were many of them involved in management? If I knew that, I could tailor my on-the-fly comments to the interests of this mixed audience.[*] So I asked:

Words That Work:
"Before we get going, so I can best tailor to this group, can I ask for a show of hands – how many here are the technical experts at their company? How many are in management?"

It took maybe 15 seconds and now I knew something about the make-up of the audience. Equally important, they knew I cared about being on target for them. You can do the same in your meeting, no matter what the size.[**]

Bigger Means Slower

In larger rooms you need to slow down because your sound waves have to go that extra distance and bounce off walls as they do. If you speak too quickly, those in the back may find it hard to understand what you're saying. To remind yourself of this, you might want to put a small note that says "SLOW!" in a spot where only you can see it.

---

[*] Just as we discussed doing in 'Mixed Meetings', in Chapter 5.

[**] You might discover useful information. One time, by asking, I learned that two visiting executives from Europe were sitting in, and I added some points specific to their markets. It led to doing workshops for them later that year.

Presenting to International Audiences

From Tokyo to Sao Paulo, I've been amazed at how salespeople have so much in common. It is, however, a mistake to present to an international audience the same way you would back home. Here are some tips for making the best impression.

Slow Down

Especially if you are speaking to a large group, but slow it down even if you're just at a trade show booth. To them, you have quite an accent, plus it takes your audience slightly longer because they're doing mental translation.

Audience Reactions Can Vary

Different cultures are often more subdued. For example, it may be considered rude in an audience to call out questions, even if the presenter asks for them.[*] In such cases, if you feel it's important to address certain commonly asked questions, be prepared to raise them yourself – so you can now answer them to the group:

Words That Work:
"Often in groups like this I'm asked…"

Leave Your Local References at the Border

For example, don't refer to miles per hour if you're in Europe or Canada; translate it into kilometers. Convert your currencies, too. Check your slides to make sure they don't only have dollar signs or

---

[*] It may also be seen as poor form to call out answers to questions the speaker poses to the group. If you don't get a reply, simply treat your question as if it were rhetorical, and answer then it yourself as if you always intended to. *"The answer is usually…"*

other US-oriented visuals. Yes, it might take a bit of effort to do this, but people notice. It shows your awareness and respect.

Watch Your Idioms

If American English is not my native language, don't count on me grasping any flip phrases. To you, the phrase "It's a no-brainer." might mean 'it's obvious'. But in London or Singapore it could just as easily be construed the opposite way, as 'a choice made by someone without any brains'. Confusion follows.

Be Careful with Humor

Humor is built upon shared experiences along with cultural norms and expectations. That gets complicated. If you are going to go for the laugh, don't be subtle or deadpan. Make the humorous situation very clear, delivering it with a big smile, so all can be sure you are joking and be confident that it's okay to laugh.

Chapter 7

Advancing
to a Higher
Version Number

Remember you, five years ago? Ten years ago?

Since then you have certainly advanced – you know more, you understand more. You've become more valuable to customers and to your company.

That's what personal advancement is all about. It determines how high a person will soar – and when.

I've long felt it shouldn't be left to chance. In this section, you will find ideas and insights about reaching further, faster. At the very end I've reprinted two of my often-requested magazine articles about success and selling.

It's our final section, and I can't think of a more important topic than you and your future success.

What Version Number are You?

In order to be competitive, every business has to constantly move forward. And so does every salesperson.

Yet so many people fail to invest in themselves – to develop skills and capabilities that will enhance their productivity and success.

I recently gave a presentation to over 2000 salespeople in Berlin, Germany. The conference was to launch the latest version of the client's technology – version 5.0. I showed a slide with their new version number, and then with a click a second line of text appeared on that slide.

It added this question: "...and What Version Number are _You_?"

I then asked my audience, _"And how about your customers – the ones you met with last week – what version number are_ they_?"_

It was clear from their expressions that I'd struck a chord.

Each year our marvelous technologies advance. Customers demand it; they won't tolerate manufacturers that don't advance their products at regular intervals.

But these new-version technologies have to be sold to old-version humans. That's asking a lot of the salespeople who are responsible for creating desire and orders.

Every technology company expects engineers to advance their skills. It is just as important that we in Sales continue to advance ours. After all, doesn't the entire company's revenue stream and future depend upon the salespeoples' insights and customer-facing skills?

----

11 Years Sales Experience?
Or One Year Repeated 11 Times?
Whenever I hear a salesperson say, "I've been doing this for 11 years" – implying they already know all there is to know – I think of my aunt Alice. She's got over 40 years driving experience. All of them lousy.

Sure, she can boast she's been doing this for decades – but my advice is to stay far away from her on the highway.

Only those who decide to continually advance become more masterful and valuable over the years.

The fact is, no one majored in Selling Technology in college; there's no such degree. Unlike accountants, lawyers or even hairdressers, there is no standard level of knowledge or skill we can expect a technology salesperson to have. There's no certification, no equivalent of version number.

"Hi, I'm Ken Wax, Version 6.3."
But imagine if we could bring version numbers to the people who sell.

When we meet I can explain all the new features and capabilities that can be found in the newest version of me. *"Oh, sure, last year's Ken Version 6.0 was pretty darn good. But since then I've learned more about several vertical industries, have developed several new tactics for selling in web-conferences and created a new speech just for mid-size tech companies who battle much larger competitors.*

And wait until you see Ken Wax Version 7.0 next year!"

Imagine how useful such version numbers would be in managing and developing people. The VP could sit down with the sales manager and ask, *"Lee is only at Version 3.2? Gee, he was Version 3.0 when we hired him two years ago. I'm concerned the sales team has been too busy and hasn't been advancing like our products and engineers are – so instead of just having product training at our sales meeting, we really need some very specific training on motivating today's customers."*

Done right, salespeople would love it. After all, with each upgrade they would make more money because they and the company are winning more deals, more often.

But it won't be happening. There's no way companies can assign version numbers to humans, which is probably a good thing.

But each of us can easily assign *ourselves* a number.

Then we can deliberately work on becoming a more advanced version by next year, or maybe even by next month. As we advance, our work – even with 'same old version customers' – delivers greater impact and results every day, week and month.

So I'd like to ask – what version number are you?[*]

---

[*] And if I ask you this same question three or six months from now, will I hear a different answer?

How Much Should a Sales Rep Know?

After speaking at a big channel event, a regional manager from Oracle asked me that question. The correct answer is: 'More'.

- *More* than your counterpart at your competitor knows.

- *More* than your customer really expects a salesperson to know.

- *More* than you knew last week, even if just by a little.

The last one is the most important. When I work with sales teams, it is quickly clear who the best salespeople are. They know more than the rest, because they never stop learning.

If you want to make more money and reach greater heights, here's the recipe: Find the time, put in the effort and learn more. Invest in yourself.

It really is that simple. Anyone can do it; no one needs to assign the task. That's how stars shine at startups, it's how top achievers outsell the rest at established companies.

All it takes is a decision, and investing 20 minutes or so a day to do it.[*]

---

[*] What can be gained in 20 minutes? It adds up. Investing 20 minutes a day equals over an hour and a half a week. That's over 75 hours a year – the equivalent of about two full workweeks. Anyone who does that is definitely going to outperform the 'too-busy' masses who don't invest in themselves.

All You Need to Know About Sales Rejection

No one likes getting rejected. But it happens all the time – even to the most successful salesperson.

Here's a secret which, if you haven't yet discovered it, just may change your life. At the very least it will save you a lot of time and frustration:

It's not you they're rejecting.

How could it be? They know practically nothing about you as a person. No inkling as to your personality, kindness, sense of humor, taste in music, hobbies, or insights.

They are merely reacting to the role you are playing in business right now. That's the only thing they can be 'rejecting'. Their decision to not embrace you and move ahead says far more about them and the internal situation at their company than it does of you.

Don't waste even a moment wallowing in it. If this prospect doesn't want to dance, move on. If there's something to learn from this experience, learn it and move on.[*]

Selling will always be about probabilities. Even the world's most skilled salesperson won't perfectly match the needs and secret issues at every interaction. Interpreting that as 'rejection' is just a waste of time that helps no one.

---

[*] In some cases you might want to move on to others within that company. Just because this person isn't interested doesn't mean the entire organization shares that view.

Avoid Tech Support Syndrome

Ever work on a tech support line? If you did, you quickly came to the conclusion that your product is terrible.

How could you not? Each day you come to work, answer the phone, and there's someone telling you your product doesn't work right.

You help them fix that problem and pick up the phone again. Yep, it's another person with a problem because your product isn't working right. And so it goes until quitting time. Tomorrow is another day – of more of this.

With such experiences day in and day out, you quickly conclude your product is weak.

Except it isn't. Over at your competitors, the same thing, more or less, is happening on *their* support lines.

The fact may be that 99.9% of your customers love your product. Only they're not calling up each day to tell you so.

The same is true when you sell. If you lose most often to one competitor, you can quickly conclude they are superhuman. But over there, where they may be losing most often to *you*, they see you similarly larger than life.

Your Credibility Counts

Pardon me for asking, but *who the heck are you*?

I really want to know – and so do your customers. But not to be polite; they want to know about you for purely selfish reasons.

Here's why: Imagine you're at a dinner party. The host announces his cousin Dan will be showing some card tricks in the den. You like magic but have little desire for some clumsy amateur magic show, so your plan is pass on it and stay where you are.

But what if instead your host had mentioned that Dan, though an amateur, is a sleight of hand expert who has studied with some of the world's greatest magicians?

Those extra few seconds of explanation change things significantly. Dan now has new credibility – and you are far more likely to get a good seat and pay close attention.

You're also more likely to be impressed with the experience. Credibility is like that. It steers our perceptions.

In selling technology, credibility is king. If I know you are an experienced expert, I'm far more likely to want to meet with you. I'm also more likely to pay attention, believe what you say and then repeat it to others. And chances improve that I'll want to have you meet others here at my company.

It's easy to overlook all this, because, well, you already know all about you. You know your experience, your training, your successes, your integrity, your follow-through, your everything.

What one has to keep in mind is that I, as a prospect, know none of that.

That's why it's useful for me to get an answer to the question: Who are *you*? Until I know more, I don't know how to value you.

Each time you meet a new prospect, there's only one thing they really know for sure: that you're here to hopefully sell them something. Since they've met plenty of mediocre salespeople in their life, their natural assumption will be that yet another one is here. It may not be fair, but it is a reasonable starting point. You would feel the same if you were in their seat.

In my workshops, I have taught thousands of salespeople how to create and deliver their own short 'credibility speech'. It's less than 30 seconds in length, but it changes everything.[*]

You need credibility. Actually, you already have it. It's just that strangers have no way of knowing. You just have to tell them. As you will see on the next page, that's what your 30-Second Credibility Speech is all about.

---

[*] I've lost count of how many times I've received emails along the lines of, "Ken, I still use the Credibility Speech I created in your workshop every day."

Introducing...You!

Most technically oriented salespeople can't imagine talking about themselves with customers. It strikes them as time wasted – it's either puffery or boasting. They're here to talk tech, so let's dive in!

Not so fast. You're here to build a relationship, aren't you?

You owe it to that prospect to explain who you are and what your value is to them. You're not boasting – you're helping them.

Your credibility is tremendously influential; it determines your impact each time you talk with customers. That's why your '30-Second Credibility Speech' is such a powerful tool.[*]

What belongs in your credibility speech?   It all depends on you and your background.

If you've been in the business for many years, you will want to highlight what you've seen and the many customers you've helped If you are new to selling, then your value comes in other ways (see next page). It may be short, but creating one's Credibility Speech is not a trivial task. It takes a lot of thought to distill one's business experience and value into 30 succinct seconds.

While it is beyond the scope of this book to guide you in crafting yours – here are some guidelines (the next section will use mine as an example of how to put them into practice):

---

[*] Many times it has even delivered results before the workshop was over. Example: The salesperson had a call previously scheduled with a marginally interested prospect. They used their new Credibility Speech – and the tone and level of interest immediately changed for the better.

Under 30 Seconds: No exceptions. Anything longer will be too much. You will want to say it out loud as you time it. If it's too long (and it will be, at first), distill it and time it again.

Set It Up Properly: You need to convey how the only reason you are telling it is to help them. If you don't fit this into the first sentence they won't know why you're doing this.

Tailor It to Your Current Strengths: It you have extensive experience, cite those companies and projects. If you don't yet have that, focus on your training, access to experts, and follow-through. Everyone has some facets of great value; it's just a matter of identifying yours.

It's Really About Them: Every phrase should give them confidence about what you can do for them and their company.

Don't Rush Through: Your tone is conversational. Imagine an experienced surgeon or accountant briefly explaining their training and experience. As you practice, say it out loud and don't rush.

Here's an interesting side-benefit to having and using a good 30-Second Credibility Speech.

Because you're revealing things about you, in many customer situations, after you've explained your background the moment is perfect for you to ask about *their* background.

Words That Work:
"Can I ask for a little on you and your background at this company, or in general?"

Most people will appreciate that you've asked and will enjoy talking about themselves. You are advancing the relationship (and you may learn things that even people who've worked with them for years do not know).

Will there be some who instead reply, *"I'd rather we just dive in to what you're here to talk about."?* Yes, but not many[*]. That's their business persona, so just move on and talk business. You've already accomplished your goal of having them know your value. (The good news about such folks is that when the time comes and they do share, you know you've reached a special status.)

You will find that it takes a surprising amount of work to craft an effective 30 second speech. But then you've got it forever, and it brings value to every single customer you meet.

if you don't do it, who will?

[*] This has only happened to me twice in my entire career.

Introducing...Me

Let me give you an example of a 30 Second Credibility Speech that will help get you started. It's a version of mine, but it will bring you ideas on how yours could flow.

Imagine we're in a meeting or phone call to discuss training, consulting or a speech. It was arranged by someone who reports to you, but we've never met before. My challenge would be to give you confidence in me and help create desire for what I offer. Here's what I might say:

"Before we start, it might be helpful to take 30 seconds for a quick tour of my experience and how it might relate to your situation.

"For over 20 years I've helped sales teams advance all over the world, at companies ranging from industry giants like IBM, Monster.com, and Microsoft, to mid-size companies and even startups.

"Everything we do is customized to your goals and specific challenges, so there's no time wasted on generic filler. You will find the focus is on specific approaches your people can put into action immediately.

"With that in mind, can I ask about what you want to accomplish?"

Time: about 25 seconds. Were you bored? I doubt it; even in the first sentence you knew it would be about benefiting your organization.

Most importantly, didn't knowing the breadth of my experience make you want to tell me more about your situation than if you didn't know that information? Big payback here – for everyone – from investing less than a half minute. (Now it's time for you to carve out the time and begin crafting yours.)

Social Media, Your Presence In

What would I find in your profile on LinkedIn?

Would I learn things that would enhance my impression of you? Or would I see a sparse list of companies and years worked?

There's no question that prospects will be checking you out. I know I would if I was considering entrusting a major project to you. I'd probably do that even if I was only considering a phone meeting.

That's why your profile there matters – it's a way to figure out your possible value to me and my company. What it conveys may determine if I invite others to our meeting, and whether my manager is on that list. Even a small detail in your profile might intrigue me and enhance your credibility – for example, if I learn that you were once a systems engineer.

Don't mistakenly think your profile is only for job searching. If you sell technology solutions, it is a powerful, leveraged tool every day. Here are five ways to leverage it:

1) Take Advantage of the 'Summary' Section on Top
Unlike the very structured employment chronology sections, here you can write anything you'd like. Use it to cite attributes that matter to customers. For example,

> *"Experienced account manager at Fortune 500 and midsize customers. Strong track record of customer satisfaction and bringing projects in on time and on budget."*

Assume it went on for another paragraph with details that bring me insights. Isn't that more confidence inspiring than merely having *"Account Manager, Software."*?

211

2) Don't Merely List Previous Employers

For each of those employers, include items of interest to prospective customers. It depends on your specifics, of course, but it's likely to help everyone if you mention things like:

- Key technologies you've sold

- Accounts you've worked with

- Industries or regions you've covered

3) Focus Attention On Things That Make You Stand Out

For example, suppose at a previous employer you were a system engineer before becoming an account manager. Call attention to this by having *two* job entries for that employer, one for each of those positions. Now anyone even glancing at your profile will see you have credentials as a techie, which may be impressive to them (especially if they are one, or have been).

To further call attention to it, begin the Account Manager entry along the lines of, *'Promoted from System Engineer to Account Manager.'*

Invest some time on your presence in social media; this is an area that will only grow more important as time goes on.

The 5 Levels of Selling

When I met my first human brochure, I didn't know what to make of him.

It was early in my career before entering the technology business, back when I was a buyer for Macy's. Because my job was to buy millions of dollars of consumer electronics, all sorts of salespeople wanted to meet with me. They ranged from local reps to National Sales Managers for leading manufacturers. It was quite an education.

I can still remember being amazed that someone would fly across the country for a meeting, only to turn pages and bring no additional value whatsoever. So many obviously knew nothing about the pressures and needs of a buyer, or how buying decisions were made.

My experiences on the 'other side of the desk' taught me much about the variances among salespeople. Meet enough salespeople and you appreciate that there are definite levels of understanding and abilities.

When I joined the tech field, it was in distribution, as a merchandise manager for Ingram-Micro. Again, I was meeting with many salespeople and their managers – and again I found those distinct levels of selling.

Each level corresponds to the value a salesperson brings to his or her customer. As I discovered when I rose to sales management positions, each also has direct correlation to how effective they are at bringing in new business and protecting existing accounts.

Level # 1: Human Brochures

This person knows various things about their company's products, services and their company's story. Just ask; they're happy to relay speeds, feeds, and details. But first, they'd like to show you the company's overview slideshow and read every bullet point. Or just talk for a very long time.

To them, selling is telling. They have a lot to say about their company's offerings; isn't that the purpose of a sales call?

Most human brochures are blissfully unaware of their limitations. Whenever a sale is lost, they know why. It was a fickle executive, incompetent contact, lying competitor, or our stupid pricing. Of one thing they are certain: It wasn't their fault.

Level #2: We're Good, They're Not

Next are those with Level #1 knowledge plus an understanding of the competition's pitch.

This is the stereotypical professional salesperson.[*] Proud of his or her company and able to point out all sorts of (alleged) competitor weakness that their company has taught them. This can be useful to the customer, who now knows what areas to probe with those other guys to get a lower price.

The biggest problem with the Level #2 salesperson is that they cost as much to hire, train and field as a higher level salesperson. Finding them leads costs just as much, and high-potential opportunities are placed in their hands. If you're going to go to all that trouble and expense, why settle for their limited impact?

---

[*] When technical people become salespeople, their understanding of selling is often Level #2. It's comfy; many never leave.

Level #3: A Bigger Picture

At this level, the salesperson has crossed over to be able to bring value. He or she has some level of historical understanding of their field and of customers. They can convey stories of how other companies have benefited, though these are limited to their first-hand knowledge of their own accounts.

The Level #3 professional knows how we all got to where we are. He or she can speak about the advances over the years, changes in standards, and all that. They can relay the experiences of others who've bought, which is instrumental if one wants to get someone excited and able to talk up a purchase inside their company.

It's easy to see how a Level #3 salesperson is more likely to influence a prospect, especially when their competitors are merely Level #1 or #2.

Level #4: Broader Knowledge & Insights

Big jump to get here. At Level #4, you have perspective – you can see the purchase from the customer's point of view[*] and you are focused on creating *desire*.

We're now entering the area where a salesperson is bringing a customer knowledge they couldn't easily get with a few clicks at your website. Their stories have Insights. They can help a prospect look smart and make a confident choice. This comes from having additional dimensions of knowledge:

- *Beyond Their Own Experience:* The salesperson at this level has taken the time to learn the stories of experiences at customers with similar challenges, even if they are in other industries.

---

[*] Yep, you're absolutely right – 'Customer Vision'

- *Industry Knowledge* – they're on top of trends and changes in that prospect's field, and what the business will look like in 12 or 18 months.

- *Buying Knowledge* – they've developed an understanding of the dynamics and behind-the-scene decisions taking place for this sale to happen.

This all combines to deliver a personal value to their contact. The Level #4 salesperson knows what questions are going to come up and what the contact needs to know to look smart. They know how to arm that contact with examples and analogies that will inspire their manager and other business executives.

Level #5: Valued Consultant

Our highest level is reserved for those who know so much they could conceivably charge for their insights. They've put in the time and effort to develop knowledge, perspective and vision that is befitting a successful consultant in the prospect's field.

At Level #5, he or she has moved beyond seeing their job as expertly pitching smart solutions. Instead, the goal is have that contact succeed and become a hero in their organization.

No one is born at Level #5. One needs to aim for it and put in work to get there. But the pay sure is better.

At every company I've worked with, the top money makers are at the higher levels. Shifting oneself up even a single level delivers a striking revenue impact.

Where Does Success Come From?

*I wrote this for a tech-industry magazine in the U.S.; it was
very popular and later reprinted on four continents. My hope
is that it has the same impact on you that it has had on
others.*

Everyone would love to be wealthy. No, we won't give up our beliefs
or joys for it, but each of us would like to be in a position of success
where we don't need to worry about money.

Yet few people get to taste wealth. Why? And what can we learn
from those who somehow achieve great things?

We can't learn much from those whose wealth come from
inheritance or owning a piece of real estate that skyrocketed. Let's
not condemn them, of course, but there's little we can do about
choosing our parents or accumulating wealth through sheer luck.
Instead, I care about those people who had to earn success by
themselves.

And I'm not the only one to care about them. During the past
century, much research has been done about remarkably successful
people. But It's not common knowledge. You can spend 18 years or
more in school and not receive a single hour-long lesson about
success. It's one of those fields you have to actively seek out.

In my work, I am fortunate to meet many successful people. Some
have started companies; others have helped their companies reach
new heights. Over the years, my company has interviewed
thousands of executives and sales professionals at various stages of
their careers.

Few fit the image we read in the self-serving autobiographies. You
know the type, in which the ghost writer tells how the "author"

217

---

knew he or she was destined for greatness while still in diapers. Such books paint the picture of an unstoppable rise, perhaps with one or two dramatic obstacles to masterfully overcome along the way. A good read, but clearly not resembling any real human we've ever met.

Real life is rarely so neat and tidy; it has no theme music. Dramatic moments happen, but they're not punctuated by chapter endings or fading to black. Ghostwriters simply use poetic license to overlook the blemishes and create 'larger than life' stories.

So why are some people more successful than others? Surprisingly it has little to do with intelligence or schooling. Many a Ph.D. is driving a taxi right this minute. And we've all heard of millionaires who dropped out of high school. You'll find little correlation between academic grades and success or happiness.

What, then, does show up again and again in remarkably successful people? Three traits do. Quest for knowledge, Setting goals, and Taking risks.

Quest for Knowledge:
In the early 1900's, Andrew Carnegie provided a fellow named Napoleon Hill with letters of introduction to other extremely successful individuals (a necessity if you hoped to get time with such people). Hill then set out to interview them, preferably in their homes.

He visited many mansions and noticed something they all had in common. A library. This wouldn't be a furniture museum with books as mere props; it would instead be an entire room filled with relevant knowledge. Indeed, from the library alone, one could easily conclude in which field that person had made his fortune.

Children in grade school spend about six hours each day learning. By college, it's down to just a few hours. Many people think they're done learning when they get out of school. They're so busy, they only learn what their boss tells them to learn. Would you buy stock in a person who's passive about their own development? Me neither.

Setting Goals:
Research has consistently shown that specific goal-setting is a trait, really a habit, of the very successful. Not pie-in-the-sky daydreaming, but clear, sensible, short and long-term goals. And they put them in writing.

That's very important. Whether your goal is to become an expert in an emerging area, win a key account or to acquire a slick car, you need to put it on paper to make it real. Thoughts disappear; putting anything in writing shows a level of commitment.

Then you have to tell someone about that goal. Not just anyone – it must be a person who believes in you and will support you as you take steps toward it.

Goals aren't easy. You could fail to reach them. Of course, people who don't set goals don't have that problem. Which brings us to our third point: The world rewards risk.

Taking Risks:
Nothing happens without taking intelligent, well-thought-out risks. And make no mistake about it: Risk means sacrifice. Setting goals isn't enough. You'll have to also decide what you're willing to give up to reach those goals.

It may be time. You may have to get to work earlier or pass on watching television some nights. It could be comfort. Venturing into areas that are new involves uncertainty, awkwardness. It's likely to require spending some money. Reaping rewards tomorrow usually requires investing something today.

There's no law forcing anyone to take risks. That's why many people don't. But keep in mind: the fruits tend to go to those who do.

Knowledge. Goals. Risks. When your great-grandchildren are your age, those will still be essential ingredients in reaching great heights in success and happiness.

The millionaires that Hill interviewed are long gone, but their mansions are still standing. Other successful people are living in them now. But they won't live forever either.

Those mansions won't remain empty; someone else will move into them. I'd like you to be one of them. Because when I move in, I'd like to have some nice neighbors.

Letter to a Young Salesperson

This article seems to touch people. I've received the most requests for reprints of it. Even the most experienced salespeople seem to enjoy it; I think you will, too.

Dear Colleague,

So you're new to selling. Welcome to a good place; one that is unique in the world of business. But it is also uniquely strange.

Many years ago, I sat where you sit now. I've learned a bit since then; these days companies even seek my counsel in this area. So I thought I'd write and offer a few thoughts.

First and foremost, our kind makes it all happen. People who sell are the engines that drive the business world. If anyone doubts this, ask them to consider a company with fine products, great warehouse staff, and brilliant executives. With enough sales, they thrive and grow. But with too few, it all withers and is soon gone.

Selling is a complex art – and it is an art. Be wary of any simplistic slogans or big promise recipes. If selling was nothing more than a formula, it would be easy. Every company would follow the recipe and become incredibly successful.

Those who don't sell have difficulty understanding it. You'll sometimes hear bright people, who may be insightful in other areas, trivialize it as being little more than talking with enthusiasm, then taking orders.

But selling is far more. To be a success, you will have to be a combination of psychologist, technical expert, historian, coach, creative thinker, project manager, and motivational speaker. Wait, it

----

gets tougher. You'll also have to know when to choose which hat to wear, and how to gracefully switch among them.

It's demanding work. Constant rejection is part of the job. Don't let this drain your energy or enthusiasm; it's nothing personal. Those people don't even know you. Try to see those "no"s as necessary, if undesired, steps along the path to your next sale.

Selling is probably the only career where you can write your own paycheck. Plenty of people, starting with less than you, have become wealthy beyond their wildest dreams through selling.

But it won't be easy. *Selling is probably the world's best-paying hard work. But it's not a very good easy job.* Accomplished salespeople can amass a fortune. But, for those whose goal in life is to cruise, it's a lot of pressure and hassles just to earn a paycheck.

Set your sites high. Work as if you were working for yourself, because you are. Figure out ways to accomplish more. Then reap the rewards of your hard work.

What does it take to be remarkably successful in selling? The first requirement is to make a decision. Decide you will be a top performer, and that you will acquire advanced skills in order to achieve this.

Always be learning. Ask questions, study those who are already achievers. Learn about your industry, its history, trends, and what people are saying about its future. Then learn as much as you can about your customer's business, not just the parts that involve your wares.

Read business books, not just the magazines that arrive for free. Read widely. A proven idea in one field is often refreshingly new and potent in another.

Two arts, those of presenting and persuading, will greatly influence your success. Master them, and you become more valuable to customers, to your company, and to yourself.

Doing all this will demand time, and that means sacrifice. Success comes to those who honestly answer this question: *What do I want, and what am I willing to sacrifice right now to get it?*

Selling means working with people, and we humans, well, can be erratic, difficult, and downright crazy at times. Be tolerant — getting upset won't change this. But your sense of humor might.

Keep it all in perspective. Never do anything that is unethical, or even on the edge. There's no need to. And life is just too short to live it that way.

Since the dawn of civilization, every great accomplishment has required selling. Without talented salespeople, no businesses have thrived, no research has earned funding, no charity has been able to help others. Nothing takes flight without those who can inform, inspire — and deliver results. Salespeople.

You are entering a noble, important career. One where the sky is the limit, and you hold the keys to your success. Allow me, on behalf of all those who have come before you, to shake your hand and say, "Welcome".

Enjoy the ride!

Ken

You are invited to share your
thoughts, questions or stories
with Ken at **www.kenwax.com**